'Robin Greenwood is now one of the most experienced and effective guides to transforming congregations and their communities. His wisdom is deeply and imaginatively biblical, centred on God and God's generous blessing, and utterly realistic about the Church and our society. He draws readers into the fullest life possible: following Jesus, living in praise and becoming a blessing. A book full of promise for the local church.'

Professor David Ford, Regius Professor of Divinity
University of Cambridge

'This is without doubt a book for our times: essential reading and essential practice for all who yearn for a better way for churches than endless initiatives, mission statements and strategies.'

The Rt Revd James Bell, Bishop of Ripon

'Robin Greenwood has done it again. *Sharing God's Blessing* offers a creative, thoughtful, clear and accessible approach to being the people of God in transitional and challenging times. It is a book rich in practical wisdom, born of seasoned experience and theological reflection. There is something for everybody and it will be particularly helpful, stimulating, and a source of blessing for the local church.'

The Rt Revd Professor Stephen Pickard, Executive Director
Australian Centre for Christianity and Culture
Charles Sturt University, Barton, Australia

'In bringing insights and practices from participatory and appreciative inquiry to church renewal, Robin Greenwood provides a practical and theologically rich approach to conversation in church communities. Conversation in these modes allows for individual and communal appreciation of God's blessing to be shared and to be the lenses through which practical issues in a local church are examined, explored and addressed. These approaches also provide the ground on which we can learn and develop rich knowledge of how to engage local churches in renewal from within.'

David Coghlan, Professor in Organization Development
Trinity College, Dublin; Co-editor of
The Sage Encyclopedia of Action Research

'This volume, with its positive contributions and practical focus on God's blessing, is full of guidelines, stories and wisdom for diocesan and local church leaders, indeed for all seeking deeper insight into God's transforming love. This book is a joy to read and a blessing.'

Dr Fredrica Harris Thompsett, Mary Wolfe Professor
Emerita of Historical Theology, Episcopal Divinity
School, Cambridge, Massachusetts

'*Sharing God's Blessing* provides a valuable resource and a process allowing a group of people very quickly to develop an atmosphere of trust, within which to ask difficult and deeply felt questions, share life experiences at an extra-ordinary level of painfulness and depth, be silent together, laugh and talk together, and discover a greater awareness of being blessed, of where God comes into our lives, and of joy in the church community. Robin Greenwood has provided a vital resource for groups of Christians to take responsibility for their own learning and to spend time exploring what really matters to particular people in specific situations.'

The Revd Louise Taylor-Kenyon, Vicar of the Parish of
Embsay with Eastby, Diocese of West Yorkshire and the Dales
and Clergy Continuing Ministerial Development Officer
in the Ripon and Bradford Episcopal Areas

'Combining the themes of group conversation with blessing has been very helpful for our young adults. It brought together a group of those desiring conversation at a deeper level. In the past we had struggled to attract people to Bible study but through this material we have developed a more intimate conversation helping us to grow in our knowledge of God and value our relationships with one another. We gained insight into how we could be a blessing to others throughout our extended church community. We shall continue the journey.'

Jill Foster, Lay Worker with Students and Young Adults
Brunswick Methodist Church, Newcastle

'This resource by Robin Greenwood takes us into new places as congregations are supported on a journey to recognize and celebrate the blessings in their life together. Here is an innovative way of exchanging and reflecting on God's ways and purposes in communal Christian living through accompanied and structured conversation. Tested in the life of churches in the UK and USA, transformational conversations are shown to be a key to growing greater intimacy with God, society, others and our deepest selves. Congregations will be refreshed and affirmed in engaging with this material. There are also signposts for how churches can move from focusing on their survival to becoming a blessing in their context.'

Canon Dr Malcolm Grundy, Visiting Fellow, York St John University

'Our church's involvement in the Participatory Action Research project leading up to the publication of *Sharing God's Blessing* has been of enormous benefit to us. Shy and often inarticulate Christians blossomed through feeling safe to share their inner thoughts and aspirations. We have grown in our recognition that a community can only be a living reality through participating – we find the courage to "work upon" ourselves and let Christ transform us. Far from being threatening, as inward change can often be, it is becoming apparent that we are finding joy through the emergence of renewed relationships with God and our church and neighbourhood.'

The Revd Martin Gilham, Parish Priest
St James, Shilbottle, Diocese of Newcastle

'*Sharing God's Blessing* combines deeply theological insight with immense practical wisdom. Particularly valuable are Robin's reflections on the role of the "companion" in enabling church communities to grow in mutual trust, understanding and confidence. These are surely marks of a community that knows itself to be blessed by God and that will be equipped to share the fruits of that blessing with others.'

The Revd Simon Cowling, Rector of Priory Church of
St Mary and St Cuthbert

'Robin Greenwood's *Sharing God's Blessing* offers an encouraging lens through which to view and review the life and mission of the local church. The discipline of putting blessings first frames thinking and conversation about God and the church in a life-giving way. The hope of blessing brings into clear focus questions around the mission and ministry of the church and positively animates church group conversations.'

The Revd Rachel Wood, Local Ministry Development Officer
Diocese of Newcastle

'Taking part in conversations on blessing has helped our church develop confidence to say what we think; to trust each other to listen; and to value what others say, even if we disagree. It has helped us to value each other more and build a community of trust, mutual responsibility and commitment.

'It has challenged us to think about what we are here for, what our mission is and what each can do to enable the vision of the church to be realized. It has empowered each of us to believe that our contribution matters. It has helped us cope with trauma and uncertainty and to accept and embrace change.'

The Revd Sarah Miller, Vicar with the wardens
of Newbiggin Hall, Newcastle

'Robin Greenwood has provided Lutherans with a resource to lead us into the study of Scripture around the theme of blessing. More than that, it opens us holistically to new ways of seeing mission and ministry through conversations on our relating both personally and as a community to the presence and activity of God. Participating in conversations on blessing has helped our church develop confidence, in affirming the gifts we have and amplifying what is possible by God's grace. At a time when many lament the loss of Christendom, Robin stimulates our church to know God's blessing more abundantly, releasing our church for further acts of compassion in our neighbourhood.'

The Revd Dr Richard O. Hill, Pastor of Hope Lutheran Church
and Dean of the Peconic Conference, Selden, New York

'From his long experience in parish and diocesan ministry, combined with two years attentive companionship to particular local churches, Robin Greenwood in this book offers companionship to all with responsibility for nurturing churches at this time. He offers approaches, encouragement, and support for finding the courage to travel slowly, listening deeply to one another in conversations of honesty. This resource encourages and demonstrates practices for churches to discover again God's healing life-giving abundance in the midst of institutional turmoil and messy personal lives. Here we are called, companioned and blessed by the God who draws us to be "beloved".'

The Revd Caroline Pascoe, Development Officer, Diocese of Hereford

'*Sharing God's Blessing* has been a real encouragement to us at the "Crooked Spire" as we explore further how God is calling us to be a blessing for each other and for our town. It has encouraged tentative Christians to become faithful, and faithful Christians to become witnesses. It has started us on a new way of working together where honesty is constructive and all have a gifting and a place.'

The Revd Patrick Coleman, Vicar of St Mary and All Saints, Chesterfield

'Reading this book filled me with joy. Above all, the sense of delight came from being reminded so comprehensively that the Beloved blesses us more than we can imagine and that we too are to be a blessing, but was replenished over and over by the practical stories, sound theology and effective tools that had been developed from a process in which the participants in ministry were at the heart. Ecumenical in scope and deeply local in focus, I look forward to using this resource to companion God's people seeking to be who they are called to be. There is indeed hope!'

Jenny Dawson, Ministry Developer, Anglican Church in Aotearoa, New Zealand and Polynesia

'Robin Greenwood continues to contribute to thinking about the future being of the Church. By combining appreciative enquiry with a deep sense of how we are blessed by God, Greenwood establishes the ground for conversations that can enable the Church to be a blessing to the community within which it finds itself. Rather than focusing on what the Church has lost and what the Church doesn't have, Greenwood supplies us with an approach that moves us forward, based on what we do have and how we are blessed by God. I look forward to seeing how this can impact the life of the Church.'

The Rt Revd John Stead, Bishop of Willochra, Australia

Dedicated to those church communities,
especially in the North-East of England,
who have generously opened their doors and
their hearts to me, feeding my imagination,
as well as my body

Robin Greenwood, William Leech Research Fellow, St John's College, Durham University, is a practical ecclesiologist. For over four decades, he has held posts in parishes, cathedrals and training teams. His most recent local church responsibility was as Vicar of St Mary the Virgin, Monkseaton, Newcastle. He is a Canon Emeritus of Chelmsford Cathedral, contributes to diocesan programmes in the UK, the USA and Australia, and has been co-director of the Edward King Institute for Ministerial Development. His many titles for SPCK include *Being Church: The Formation of Christian Community* (2013), *Being God's People: The Confirmation and Discipleship Handbook* (2011), *Parish Priests: For the Sake of the Kingdom* (2009), *The Ministry Team Handbook: Local Ministry as Partnership* (2000) and *Transforming Priesthood: A New Theology of Mission and Ministry* (1994). His wife Claire is also an Anglican priest, and they are parents to Peter, Tim and Katherine and seven grandchildren.

Also by Robin Greenwood

1988 *Reclaiming the Church*, Collins
1994 *Transforming Priesthood: A New Theology of Mission and Ministry*
1999 *Practising Community: The Work of the Local Church*
2000 *The Ministry Team Handbook: Local Ministry as Partnership*
2002 *Transforming Church: Liberating Structures for Ministry*
2005 *Power: Changing Society and Churches* (with Hugh Burgess)
2006 *Local Ministry: Story, Process and Meaning* (with Caroline Pascoe)
2006 *Risking Everything: Growing Communities of Love*
2009 *Parish Priests: For the Sake of the Kingdom*
2011 *Being God's People: The Confirmation and Discipleship Handbook* (with Sue Hart)
2013 *Being Church: The Formation of Christian Community*

(All except the first on this list are published by SPCK.)

Sharing God's Blessing

How to renew the local church

ROBIN GREENWOOD

First published in Great Britain in 2016

Society for Promoting Christian Knowledge
36 Causton Street
London SW1P 4ST
www.spck.org.uk

British Library Cataloguing-in-Publication Data
A catalogue record for this book is available from the British Library

ISBN 978–0–281–07215–6
eBook ISBN 978–0–281–07216–3

Typeset by Graphicraft Limited, Hong Kong
First printed in Great Britain by Ashford Colour Press
Subsequently digitally printed in Great Britain
eBook by Graphicraft Limited, Hong Kong

Produced on paper from sustainable forests

Contents

Foreword

This is without doubt a book for our times: essential reading and essential practice for all who yearn for a better way for churches than endless initiatives, organizational readjustments, mission statements and strategies. In many places I encounter churches with a mood of 'hanging on in there', and too many Christian communities appear to live out of a sense of deficit, inadequacy, insufficiency – what Robin Greenwood calls 'the myth of scarcity'. Recovering the recognition of blessing is to regain the capacity to live out of sufficiency, abundance, surfeit and grace. 'God has given us all that we need', as Samuel Wells repeatedly affirms in *God's Companions*. 'To you is given the secret of the Kingdom of God', declares the Lord, and Robin invites us through themes of blessing, conversation and story to embrace that gift and 'use processes that release the energy of the whole Church'.

We are offered a realistic, eye-witness account of where we are at, not least the 'difficult environment for faith', but with a refreshing and energizing focus on the grace and gifts of God, showered on his people in Jesus and the outpouring of the Spirit. As always, Robin goes to the heart of the matter, and the heart of the matter for grasping the possibilities of God's future is conversation – with God, with the Scriptures, with one another. If they are to take the responsibility entrusted to them in baptism, Christian people need to articulate for themselves what it feels like to be living in the contexts they inhabit and an increasingly secular culture, and what God might be saying to his Church in these times. We are pointed to 'growing habits of conversation-based transformation'. Some of us live with the vivid memory of how shared conversations, in which members of the General Synod learned to regard one another as persons deserving attention and respect, transformed the process leading to the passing of the legislation for the ordination of women as bishops. Robin offers the philosophy, process, practicalities and motivation for such transformative conversations locally.

Stories of transformation emerge, like the one from a Christian community of which it is said, 'they've decided to stop living in the tomb created for laity centuries ago', stories of churches that have participated in Action Research conversations, informed by Appreciative Inquiry, and found themselves surprised by the guidance and grace of God released through the engagement and encounter.

Not surprisingly from the author of *Transforming Priesthood* and so many other reflections on the themes of ministry and community, there is a very welcome focus on the corporate reality of being Church, being Christian, being disciples of Jesus, which, of course, requires a new appreciation of the need for collegial habits and practices in the leadership of the Church. Also, as one might expect from such an exponent of Trinitarian theology, there is the offer of a renewed appreciation of the practice of hospitality, at the heart of the Christian gospel and yet so much neglected in the Church of the west, manifesting so much of the individualism and social divisions of the culture. Through the whole, to be sure, the reader will encounter the call of the Trinity into mutual regard and attention, to the love that offers life endlessly.

If the Reform and Renewal programme is vital as a response to the challenges of our times from the national institutions of the Church of England, *Sharing God's Blessing* may be even more significant as a resource for the renewal of the local church. I should rejoice to see its theory and practice widely used in the Ripon Episcopal Area! Profound and practical, insightful and accessible, this book will I am sure be a blessing to those who use it to find themselves becoming the blessing God has called them to be.

The Rt Revd James Bell, Bishop of Ripon

Thanks

This book is a contribution to reframing the culture, identity and confidence of churches in the light of God's blessing. It springs from engaging with many local churches and their leaders – their everyday living, hopes, traumas, griefs and delight, in the light of God's blessing. I gladly own debts of gratitude to many people and churches who have contributed or made this project possible. To the William Leech Foundation for funding my tenure of a Research Fellowship in the period 2013–15. To those who have allowed me to be part of their lives and have given me generous hospitality. To the Newcastle upon Tyne Church of England Institute Trust and to St John's College, University of Durham. To the Durham University Centre for Social Justice and Community Action committed to the systemic change of institutions.

To churches and clergy that have travelled closely with me in this project and 'road-tested' parts of this book, especially St Wilfrid's, Newbiggin Hall, Brunswick Methodist Church, Newcastle, St Thomas Aquinas and Holy Family, Darlington and St James, Shilbottle. Also for road-testing some of this material, to Hope Lutheran Church, Selden, New York, St Mary and All Saints, Chesterfield, The Priory Church of St Mary and St Cuthbert, Bolton Abbey, the United Benefice of Barnoldswick with Bracewell, All Saints, Hurworth, The United Benefice of Christchurch, Skipton with Carleton, St Peter's Addingham, and the parish of St Mary's Embsay with Eastby. To the clergy and laity in those churches and all whose responses to drafts of this material have made a difference to its accessibility and design. To fellow 'companions' for supporting me and churches through this period: Peter Kenny, Pat Moran, Diane Westmorland and Rachel Wood. To Arthur Frances, Colin Gough, Richard Hill, David Russell, Louise Taylor-Kenyon and Diane Weaver for permission to quote from their accounts of events. To former colleagues at St Mary's Monkseaton, and especially to Sue Hart for technical and design support during the trialling of some of this material. I have been grateful to Brunswick

Church also for their generous hosting of gatherings of churches involved in learning process.

In addition, for the stimulus to develop themes in this book I should like to offer appreciation of the bishop, pastors and members of the New York Synod of the Evangelical Lutheran Church in America (ELCA), the Metro New York Chapter of the Society of the Holy Trinity, together with the clergy and people of the Western Nassau Conference of the ELCA, the Anglican-Lutheran Society 2014 Conference in Budapest and the International Anglican Symposium on Shared Ministry, San Antonio, 2015.

To Claire, my wife, also an Anglican priest, for her companionship in this venture and her insights, challenges and practical skills in the field of group consultancy and psychodynamic process. To Tim Greenwood, my son, educational psychologist, for his advocacy of Participatory Action Research methodology and autoethnographic approaches to cultural change (<livingsystems.org.uk>). And to the Rt Revd Frank White, Assistant Bishop in the Newcastle diocese. To David F. Ford for encouragement throughout this project and conversations on blessing, and to Stephen Pickard for a shared commitment to identifying step changes for a renewed ecclesiology. To Malcolm Grundy for his consultancy and expertise in church development theory and practice. And to Malcolm Guite for permission to quote his poem 'Benedict' and song 'Angels Unawares'.

Finally, to SPCK editors Tracey Messenger and Rima Devereaux, for their encouragement and assistance with the more effective shaping of the book.

A five-minute video in which I introduce the themes of this book is to be found on my YouTube channel under Sharing God's Blessing. The ethos of the book is captured symbolically in the cover design. It suggests that churches are blessed to share in the work of the Trinitarian God, whose Son was stretched out on the tree of the cross, to release blessing for the whole world.

To give readers a chance to relate to me their experiences, I have set up a new email account, <sharinggodsblessing2016@gmail.com>.

Introduction: purpose and leading themes

> I believe we can change the world if we start listening to one another
> again. Simple, honest, human conversation. Not mediation, negotiation,
> problem-solving, debate or public meetings. Simple, truthful conversation
> where we each have a chance to speak, we each feel heard and we each
> listen well.
>
> (Wheatley 2002, p. 3)

Churches that are alert and eager to serve God's liberating action
in the world can't help but move from crisis to crisis. Chaos will be
routine; stability an occasional luxury. Churches that consciously live
in God's generous freedom don't take this amiss but expect every
moment to be a critical point at which to be stretched through discerning God's purposes and gifts. This book is offered as a resource
to churches, regionally and locally, in a time of reorientation. It takes
wise and creative blessing as a leading theme in the continued search
for transformative ways of being Church for the sake of the kingdom
of God. Faced with the unsustainability of many inherited patterns
of Church, the temptation is to fall into pathos rather than seek to
regenerate patterns of mission and ministry to transform people and
places. The title *Sharing God's Blessing* is a reminder of how much the
rich scriptural concept of blessing is urgently needed at this time. It
offers a counterbalance to reductionist notions and practices of community and leadership. This is not to make a naïve connection of blessing
with freedom from pain, poverty or illness. Rather it is an invitation to
put the uncertain conditions of human living within the wider horizon
of the risen Jesus' promise that in the gifts of the Holy Spirit there is
no limit to the great things his followers will do. Fertile churches know
how deeply they are blessed and the abundance that flows through a
life of blessing God. Blessing is the power for living to the full.

As will emerge, I also write from the conviction that consultancy
or companionship in church conversations, with the particular insights
of Participatory Action Research and an Appreciative Inquiry approach,

has potential to support a renewed expectation of experiencing life, not as demoralizing or dependency-creating but as within the energy field of God's blessing. For an overview of answers to the question 'Why Action Research?', see the edited collection of experience, common themes and commitments by Mary Brydon-Miller (2003), Director of the University of Cincinnati's Action Research Centre. Participative and unpredictably mutual understandings of 'blessing' – between God, creation, humanity, churches, societies and people – offer a disruptive and healing alternative to the muted panic so frequently endemic in churches today.

This book exists because of the privilege I have had, as William Leech Research Fellow, of walking closely with a cluster of churches, ecumenically, in the North-East of England, and beyond. The fruits of this research are offered to all leaders and leadership teams seeking to know how churches might live more purposively and gracefully for God's coming reign. I understand by 'leaders' all in publicly tested and commissioned church roles and all who attempt to follow their baptismal calling and sending within everyday work or in the building up of God's people. My intention is to encourage readers to join the company of 'tempered radicals'. By this I mean those who persistently demand that churches make a better job of our Christian life, gathered and dispersed, for the sake of the kingdom, but mostly from a deep affection and gratitude for what Church has given to us and a recognition of the complexities within which mainstream churches are summoned to live.

Using the book

The shape of the book is as follows:

Part 1 explores the purpose, methodology and benefits of transformational conversations on blessing. Part 2 leads groups through five structured conversations. Part 3 offers examples from experience of a variety of ways of holding church conversations, large and small, on specific occasions. It also contains some reflections by participants in this research project on the benefits of engaging with the twin themes of blessing and conversation. Its purpose is to grow confidence in embedding in church development a conversational rather than adversarial practice.

Across the world, traditional churches vary in their adaptivity to very different and new circumstances. Changing the culture and habits of being Church is proving challenging and – for some – overwhelming. This resource is designed to support the exploration of God at work in particular situations, in relation to the wider Church and world. It is an antidote to despair, hesitancy and the fearful guarding of a past inheritance.

My real desire is that you will now be convinced that you and your colleagues would benefit from reading this book together or discussing possible responses together once each has read it.

The Introduction explains why I came to write the book as I have, briefly introducing leading themes. Part 1 invites church leaders and leadership teams to engage with the theology of blessing and the possibilities for transformational conversation. Unlike discussion (which has its place sometimes), the attentive listening of conversation moves away from combative speech. Slow and respectful conversation brings us fully into *presence* with God, one another, society and ourselves. Here you will find encouragement and ideas to persuade your church to take time to talk together and so to grow a way of being Church as a beloved community that shares in God's blessing of the whole creation. I recognize that the term 'community' always needs qualifying. It can seem naively utopian unless we notice how communities can be recognized, for example as established, emergent, potential, hierarchical, divided or transient. Scripture shows often that when people and groups respond to the invitation to become God's people, risky – often turbulent – community emerges. The ordering together of community life as love is often characterized by chaos rather than stability. My experience is that the more churches dare to live in a chaordic ethos of praise, wonder, hospitality, face-to-face encounter, gratitude, laughter (in other words, 'blessing'), the more easily they move beyond the habits of pathos and resistance. As they move more confidently, they naturally enter into their role as a key agent of blessing in their locality and beyond.

Part 2 – available separately on the SPCK website as a free download at <www.spckpublishing.co.uk/free-downloadable-extract-from-sharing-gods-blessing> – offers five structured conversations for groups to learn to listen more deeply to God and to one another, grow in a sense of their church being upheld, resolve intractable problems and be challenged by God's blessing.

Conversation is, by definition, an emotional experience. It may involve dialogue, but above all, it will move us as people to a different emotional place than that which we occupied before the conversation. What happens subsequently is our choice. We may choose to act differently, or we may not, but we will have experienced something different.

(Lewis et al. 2008, p. 72)

Part 3 uses a variety of very different case studies of participative learning events I have devised and used as a further stimulus to embedding transformational conversation as a way of unleashing new power and confidence in local churches.

Making plans for group conversations

Chapters 6–11 offer five practical outlines to get your church started on conversations on blessing. This is an invitation to make this work in your particular locality. So the suggested outlines are not set in stone. A key intended benefit is for your church to gain confidence through working out how to use this material, how much of it and over what period of time. So this is deliberately not an off-the-peg course to be used without adaptation to local circumstances. The outlines benefit from having been 'road-tested' by churches and critiqued by churches of different denominations, in the UK and the USA. In Part 3 I have noted how some churches have developed their own ways of using this material.

When we merely discuss, think and plan at a surface and rational level, we are limiting our capacity to accomplish strategic goals or behavioural change. The practical organizational research of Robert Kegan and Lisa Lahey suggests that doing 'what makes sense', however compelling as an idea, is not enough to help us cross critical thresholds: 'We must also experience sufficient need or desire, visceral feelings – which is why we say they come from the gut' (Kegan and Lahey 2014, p. 210).

Encountering God and one another in conversation that includes feelings and actions helps us venture into being more *present*, in a new transformative place, escaping 'the tidy prison of small certainties' (McIntosh 2008, p. 16).

Walking with churches that, through being more fully *present* to one another and to God, I have seen them dare to recognize their gifts and respond to God's call more fully. Through participating deeply, all of us can be drawn away from mechanistic and transactional ways of thinking, feeling and doing. Choosing inclusive and mutually respectful paths helps us to begin to hear our own distinctive voice, growing in confidence and purposefulness (see Mary Oliver's poem 'The Journey' – <http://peacefulrivers.homesteads.com> or <www.goodreads.com>).

What is your church's critical question today?

The conversations outlined in Part 2 also include the chance to take a fresh look at a particular critical question that leaders and church councils may be facing. A conversation-based approach to a knotty problem can often bypass issues that discussion has been unable to resolve. By 'critical question' I mean, for example:

- the range of worship you offer;
- your contact with younger families;
- the possibilities of working with a local school;
- anxieties about finance;
- urgent issues of poverty or crime locally;
- an apparent shortage of 'ministers';
- how to contribute to improving pride in this area;
- asking how far your baptism policy is working;
- matters of justice, e.g. local housing provision, support for asylum seekers;
- your church's involvement in the wider world;
- the need to redevelop or close a building;
- how your church connects with people, organizations and different faith groups locally;
- how to develop the faith of the congregation;
- what is blocking energy in your church's mission;
- how you could help find a greater sense of liveliness in the local neighbourhood.

It may be that churches working through this material may prefer to wait and see what critical questions are generated by the group conversations and so build confidence for churches to explore them later.

Part 3 offers stimulus and resources to explore how your church can continue to mature through pursuing the habits of conversation. You will discover there further examples of and suggestions for conversations accompanied by a companion, designed to re-vision the life and mission of churches and teams. I hope this will support the opening of journeys where the seemingly impossible erupts into the newness that is God's blessing.

Taking an honest look

Despite the 'success' of a minority of churches that buck the trend, honesty demands the recognition of how hard a road is currently faced by churches, clergy and all Christian leaders. At the institutional level, the websites of denominations and dioceses tell of upbeat responses to the challenges of today. For example, the Church of England's 2015 programme 'In Each Generation: A Programme for the Renewal and Reform of the Church of England' (GS 1976) emphasizes the whole Church's call to be open to God's Spirit, to expect personal and institutional renewal and to look realistically at areas of church life that call for change. Further exploration and policies are being followed through in the four key areas of: the discernment and nurture of those called to positions of wide responsibility; resourcing ministerial education; the future development of resources; the simplification of procedures. A update document (GS 1124) summarizes the Church of England's commitment to nurturing and discerning future leaders:

> The main themes of this work are: developing a prayerful cadre of bishops and deans – confident leaders and evangelists releasing energy for mission and growth; leadership in the Church and in the nation; developing collaborative teams – both lay and ordained; enhancing management skills to oversee resources, structures and people; supporting individual formation in ministry, life and prayer; and developing a diverse pool of those who may be called to posts of wider responsibility in the near future and in years to come.
>
> (General Synod 2015, GS 1124, para. 16)

The Church of England, having surveyed experiences of ministry, continues to generate further research. One strand of this relates to assessing the effectiveness of specifically identifying and reviewing the particular roles to which clergy are called (Clinton 2014). A five-year process of research and consultation has been inaugurated to discover what best sustains clergy in their roles. Critical issues around spiritual growth, numerical growth, clergy engagement, clergy burnout and perceived diocesan support and justice are being addressed.

Again at the time of writing, the Church of England is investing resources in facilitated conversations on human sexuality: 'Given the significant changes in our culture, in relations to human sexuality, how should the Church respond?' (<www.sharedconversations.org>). These are current examples of a conscientious and rigorous approach to a widespread crisis in how churches function in a society increasingly formed by postmodern ways of speech, action and communication. It's a reminder that it's simply not productive to ignore conflict, attempt to control or fall into panic.

But we're also so very late and no one could say we haven't seen this complex crisis of credibility coming. The general run of congregations are still over-reliant on a handful of heroic leaders to wrestle with, live and teach the meaning of the gospel. In my experience the majority even of regular church attenders are not easily persuaded to deepen the intensity of their knowing and being known by God as purposefully present in the whole of living. Ecumenical publishing on mission, Church and ministry over the past 50 years has appealed for honesty to share the reality and share the responsibility for finding how to be Church differently, but while we have apparently just enough money, and just enough clergy (despite the huge dependency on the retired), we are loath to grasp the nettle.

It seems so hard for 'senior' leaders to admit the state we're in. In making appointments or preaching at induction services it would be such a relief to hear it said by a bishop or archdeacon:

We're all well aware that this is a tough time to be a church leader. Of course we all want the new vicar to be busy, effective, resilient, inexhaustible in pastoral care, a person who gives time to prayer, brilliant with youth and known in every home in the town. Yet we know how much the congregation expects of her in administration, in representing the Christian faith in schools and sorting out problems in the churchyard. So how can I, your bishop or archdeacon, share the excitement with the anxiety and support you in finding the resources to grow up in Christ, in faith, in maturity and in a willingness to stop *coming to church* and instead *to become Church*?

The reality of a widespread shaky self-esteem and lack of direction is hard to bear, and perhaps even harder to put into words. Certainly dioceses usually provide a listening ear and even counselling sessions for local leaders who are overstressed and 'failing' – in their own eyes as well as in the eyes of inherited expectation. But it's time to recognize that it's the system that's broken. This is so hard to bear for those who have given their lives for the continued healthy development of churches. For too long hard-working efficient clergy have given their all to keep the show on the road – and in so doing have perpetuated a culture of dependency – in terms of personal faith, church organization, mission and evangelism. Those of us who are 'retired' and lead Sunday liturgies are masking the situation and perpetuating a culture overdue for replacement.

See the 'Vacancies' columns of church newspapers. So often the subtext seems to be, 'Come and be a strong Christian for us; come and do our mission and ministry.' This is not to blame anyone. It's simply the result of being too loyal to our heritage. Historians know that patterns of Church and ministry are constantly evolving. The late-nineteenth-century one we're still operating by default is no longer fit for purpose. It's causing serious pain, well beyond a sticking-plaster resolution. In my consultancy work it is not uncommon for a diocesan officer to express frustration in words such as these:

I am meeting with many clergy who feel overburdened, under-resourced and lacking anyone in their congregation who can help them. I know that there are high levels of stress and of potential conflict, some of which comes from the model of the lone omnicompetent cleric and an inability to see beyond that model. I am interested in doing more to help clergy and 'senior' staff see the potential for conflict in many different circumstances and how to manage it before it becomes obtrusive. I see a disturbing level of long-term illness in clergy (and their spouses). We need to move beyond merely mechanistic and rational approaches to find positive energy.

What now demands our urgent attention?

How many of the following statements ring true in your experience?

- The faith we profess is mocked as credulous and irrelevant.
- Our churches are having to find a new place in society – on the edge.
- Churches are experiencing losses in membership, especially among younger generations.
- We don't talk about or expect much of God.
- There's an increasing sense that religion does not have a role in shaping the way society works.
- A long-overdue storm is brewing for churches.
- Clergy and other leaders we know are stressed through trying to 'keep the show on the road'.
- Only an ecumenical Church, and one that respects all faiths, can serve God's mission today.

Everyone will be able to compile their own list, but wherever I go I find churches urgently seeking to renew their practice in a difficult environment for faith.

From failure and lament to anticipation

Daring to recognize how much church life today is battered, bereft and vulnerable takes courage – personal and communal. Organizational responses must be complemented by a deep inner response to God's perpetual call, beyond the collapse of the conventional domestic arrangements of our churches. Whatever the 'glory days' of our Church in the past, the Holy Spirit has new steps for us to take today. Yet we lament the passing of cherished old ways. Naturally we grieve for a Church that is rapidly disappearing. After all, as a walk around any parish church reveals, many of us have long invested our time, energy and resources for love of the body of the Church of which we are a part. It's easy to overlook that the inherited practices of churches are just a few generations old and that patterns of church life over centuries live and then die to make way for resurrection. Otherwise they become monsters, alienated from their environment, unable to communicate and eventually made more monstrous through the negativity projected on them by others.

So local churches can still feel aggrieved that there is no longer a stipendiary priest or minister for each place. I often hear the outrage expressed like this:

> Church was just something you could take for granted. It was there when you needed it, holding steady when we faced tragedy and bereavement or celebrated new birth and marriage.
>
> Are you seriously telling us we have to take responsibility for making church happen ourselves? Surely that's why we have clergy!

Without doubt we cannot move on until we have paused to lament and give thanks for all that has been. For those now in later life, the traditions, word, sacrament, liturgies, clergy and buildings of our churches have nurtured and shaped our lives. We must allow a little time for appreciating what is passing away and noticing our sadness. It takes some maturity to avoid blaming someone for the state we're in. But we cannot linger here for too long. Loyalty to our ancestors doesn't help us serve God's mission today. We are waking up to the reality that the identity and direction of churches is too important to be left to clerical 'experts'.

The primary task is not about the survival of Christian faith or churches as institutions within a secular culture. Churches have to take time to listen and struggle to know, in ever-new circumstances, how to demonstrate the abundance, love and freedom of God for the sake of the whole creation. The way ahead may remain unclear but Christian communities are formed by opening ourselves to encounter with God as shown to us intensely in the self-sharing life and death of Jesus.

Even when the need is accepted by a critical mass of people, changing the practices and structures of being Church can prove very challenging. This is why the continual re-energizing of churches requires engagement with a wide range of disciplines, many of them familiar to congregations through their work in hospitals, business, charities and education.

In terms of Christian discipleship, deep immersion in scriptural texts and narratives reminds us how they have over centuries been continually reread with fresh imagination. Consider for example how much Scripture is constantly reworked through the work of hymn and song writers, glass artists and poets. Hoping beyond facts and circumstances is how God's people come through failure and lament towards a fresh reading:

> as we live, work, interpret, and believe in a society that is coming unglued, the church stands before the text to listen for a disclosure that is a genuine alternative to the defining power of technological consumerism, precisely because it is only in that genuine alternative that energy, power, and authority for missional initiative will be given.
>
> (Brueggemann 2002, p. 89)

A distinctive feature of this resource is the aim to hold together experience, Scripture, faith and an awareness of our everyday context to build and encourage more confident local churches. It also aims to go beyond discussion, to risk genuine and arresting encounter between one another and God. Working, as it were, from the inside as well as the outside, it seeks to develop Christian communities as companies of blessed, missional disciples.

> The very idea that in order to get better at teamwork, we *must* engage in a special kind of fighting or arguing with one another is a reason people partly dread being assigned to new teams or projects. The language [of *storming*] shapes powerful, often self-fulfilling prophecies.
>
> (Whitney et al. 2004, p. 3; emphasis in original)

As will unfold later, my intention here is to interweave the two notions of blessing (theological) and Appreciative Inquiry (organizational development) through growing habits of conversation-based transformation.

Experience and Scripture reveal how God continually lures us into newness. Jesus' gospel of repentance asks us to look again, turn around and see the world, even the most broken and self-damaging parts, as fired up with blessing. We are not called to remain in the negativity created by past mistakes and avoidance of God. We are called into knowing we live in blessing. Blessing, a key scriptural concept with many layers, reminds us of God's unique, persistent, unconditional love and desire for each human being and every part of creation.

Churches lose energy by devising plans and strategies when they are disconnected from an intense encounter with the divine through silence, meditation or worshipping together. Rather than trying to fit the newness and abundance we find in Jesus and the Holy Spirit into our previous ideas and experience, we could choose the very opposite. Suppose instead, as churches, we were humbly to recognize the limits of our understanding of the world and of God's ways within it. That could release us to give central place to knowing God, as one who comes humbly in the person, crucifixion and resurrection of Jesus Christ and the outpouring of his Spirit at Pentecost.

Here is an invitation for congregations to discover the truest character that we are baptized to become: to live primarily from knowing we are blessed by the God who crucially is present in the whole of life.

Present to God, society, one another and ourselves

Christian mission takes as its pattern Jesus' own ways of relating. We do this by rereading Scripture so as to absorb Jesus' invitation to recognize our threefold dependence: on one another (John 19.25–29); on the stranger (Luke 10.25–37); and so ultimately on the God he knew and proclaimed as *Abba* (Mark 1.9–11). A characteristic of Christian conversation is to be *present* – to God, to society, to one another and to our deepest selves where God dwells. This means spotting and letting go of the common habits of just waiting for the other to stop speaking so we can make our point, hurting one another under the guise of humour, seeking to prove ourselves right and the other wrong and belittling one another.

The wisdom of the Christian tradition is that we learn together; we make a space for the other in our hearts and minds. This is a mutual art to be acquired – one in which we all carry responsibility for recognizing each other's dignity as God's beloved. As we shall explore later, group conversations need to include ways of protecting each person where love falls short.

Such conversations are seeds of a Church where we can dare to be vulnerable enough to encounter God and one another deeply. In so doing we show the world how to live from and nurture in others the God-given birthright of human dignity. We focus on meeting others

as mature and equal in every way. This is only possible through the virtue
of humility or vulnerability, walking the self-giving way of the cross.

Listening to stories

A key practice to demonstrate this virtue will be to choose to listen
to the stories of others, locally and more widely in the world and
Church. Taking time to hear the particular way others tell the story
of a place or community can be a deep source for change.

The Armenian–American artist and photographer Nina Katchadourian,
in her series 'Uninvited Collaborations with Nature', tells a story
against herself that invites us to investigate our assumptions about
what we regard as essential interventions. In the late 1990s she began
to search out around her neighbourhood spider's webs that were damaged and to 'repair' them with red sewing thread. She illustrates her
story with beautiful photographs of the webs 'fixed' with glue or even
with the spider's own stickiness. She acknowledged that she often
caused more damage through clumsiness. She got the message, though,
when morning after morning on the ground she discovered piles of
discarded red threads. At first she had thought this was the work of
the breeze. Finally she recognized that the spider had rejected her
'help' and made an excellent repair using its own methods (<www.
ninakatchadourian.com/uninvitedcollaborations/transplant.php>).

Companions of group conversations can help a group recognize the
vital difference between accounts of how things did happen, should
happen or will happen. Also, conversation groups need to be relaxed
about the reality that a particular 'account' of events may not be the
same as 'what happened'. The companion may be able to help a group
move away from a cycle of repeated narrative of past events that limits
the emerging future. If the companion can help a group accept that
several different accounts *between them* hold fragments of 'the reality',
new and alternative stories can evolve about the future that are not
thought of as a betrayal of the past.

Listening to stories may:

- help us understand others more than we have done before;
- show us unvoiced aspects of life and communities;

- reveal that we can experience the same events quite differently from others;
- allow us to understand how something that is not difficult for us is a genuine problem to another;
- bring to life our relationship with other people and groups.

Telling our story within the account Jesus has given us of the Trinitarian God subverts the dominant culture of individualism and rank competition. The constantly unsettling questions are: 'Who is the God we worship?'; and 'Are we willing to be called as servants and friends of this God made known in Jesus?' This book is designed to be a support to loyal critics, generous rebels and pioneers of renewed Christian community.

Ministry as partnership

The – imaginary – watermark in the paper of this book proposes that we seek ways to transform the operational theology of Church on the basis that all Christians can act in partnership instead of competition. As Christ's body, our common vocation is to have an impact for creative love and reconciliation within our immediate neighbourhood and personally to be an infectious influence for Christ. Let's assume that for most of us our share in Christ's work is in the ordinary places where we struggle to live responsibly and spend most of our time.

If we are every bit as much Church when we are dispersed as when we are occasionally gathered, then we need to be actively resourced to be fully Church wherever we are. A primary question to ask of all of us who participate in Church is: 'What are you doing most of the week?' Paying attention to the range of our personal responsibilities in the whole of life is a priority for individuals as well as for the health of the local church.

Antidote to pathos

This resource is offered as an invitation to churches, whatever their situation, to recognize and be thankful, moment by moment, for how much God gives to enable us to become agents of radiating God's life in the world. Today few churches would deny their sense of fragility. The themes in this book propose an alternative to self-pity, despair and apathy. Churches are often overwhelmed by an internal sense of deficit and a lack of positive reception in the places where they are set. My intention is that the processes and attitudes portrayed and advocated here may be valuable to groups of local Christians and to clergy and leadership groups to encourage them to uncover their deepest resource and energy through:

* worshipping and living in God's blessing;
* growing as a Christian community;
* sharing the gospel through connecting with others;
* listening more deeply to others;
* spending time with those who find it hard to count their blessings;
* responding to the needs of those we encounter;
* introducing conversation-based transformation;
* cooperating with local churches;
* becoming a blessing to the neighbourhood;
* demonstrating hospitality and friendship;
* resourcing ministry teams;
* holding together through a time of change;
* discerning God's wisdom;
* embracing the gifts of a new leader;
* keeping faith through a time of trauma.

Twin themes: blessing and conversation

Blessing is the leading scriptural and theological theme in this book. As will unfold, my passion is that local churches will rediscover themselves as communities of God's beloved: blessed and to become a blessing, and to work for the final beatitude of all creation. Churches that – despite any failings and lack of zest – know themselves to be beloved and blessed by God generate healing and a new sense of identity. This movement between being a blessing and receiving blessing is not neat or linear but, as God's life of mutual love, completely unpredictable, as a wind that blows where it will.

The main title of the book, *Sharing God's Blessing*, comes from my reading of Mark's Gospel account of Jesus healing the woman who had suffered haemorrhages for 12 years. It ends with Jesus declaring: 'Daughter, you took a risk of faith, and now you're healed and whole. Live well, live blessed! Be healed of your plague' (Mark 5.34 *The Message*). A recurring theme will be of church communities expecting, knowing and growing in and through God's blessing and being drawn into becoming a blessing for others. I shall be exploring this relationally, as an 'ecology', rather than as a reinforcement of solo, one-way, hierarchical authority and power.

A second potent theme of the book is to explore the potential for transforming communities through intimate conversation and face-to-face encounter. In conversations I have had in churches recently there is a growing sense that it's of little use telling people *about* God when what they want is to *know* God and to be assured of this God's acceptance and blessing. In many human disciplines today, as well as in theology, we find a cultural turn towards prioritizing *presence*, *immediacy* and *relating* as a counterbalance to observation, rationalizing and a separation between theory and practice.

The desire for immediacy

These mirroring themes of blessing and conversation are vital ingredients in our understanding of the promise of fullness of life given by Jesus throughout his ministry and to his Church now. Together they find a deep resonance with the call to share in the Trinitarian God's mission in our own cultural climate. Every day at every scale of human living, we live with the dilemma that relating and networking are increasingly given priority, and yet Western societies make choices that prioritize the privacy, isolation and independence of individuals and families. Christian theology and practice of community, interdependence, friendship, mutual care, collaboration and participation bring both a gift and a challenge to dominant societal aspirations.

My presentation of both blessing and conversation seeks a creative engagement with movements in secular disciplines and in theology that witness to the abundance of God in all things, never merely repeating old truths but always drawn by the Spirit in ways that are mutually fruitful, intersecting and enlarging of the human spirit. The late Dan Hardy, an Anglican theologian, wrote of 'being attracted into the fullness of God'. He named it:

> granulation: it reaches down that deep. That's the redemptive side: that filtering goes all the way down, far more down than people realize . . . Letting be in a very real sense, something springing up. Letting one's own fullness come out.
>
> (Hardy, Ford and Ochs 2010, p. 118)

Blessing and conversation are two sides of the coin of the contemporary search for *immediacy* rather than distant or objective information *about* things. From long experience in the sphere of organizational management, Otto Scharmer, in *Theory U* (2009) shows how groups and organizations can develop leadership capacities to create a future that would otherwise be unavailable. In a time of general institutional failure, with negative consequences for communities and individuals and the degeneration of organizational effectiveness, Scharmer offers a visionary and intentional way of working together that emerges when time is taken for conscious *presencing* to emerge. It is not until those in a group facing a difficult task have the courage to be consciously and genuinely *present* that a breakthrough to newness can emerge.

Again, Margaret Wheatley – President of the Berkana Institute, a virtual organization living and working throughout the USA (<http://berkana.org>) – and her colleagues create intimate learning journeys designed for local communities to create healthy futures using their own hearts, hands and relationships. In *Walk Out, Walk On,* Wheatley tells many stories of healthy and resilient communities that have 'trusted themselves to find their own solutions and take control of their own future . . . in issues such as food, economics, education, leadership and environmental changes' (Wheatley 2011, p. 7). She lists some of the turns that have unleashed respectful human creativity across local communities from South Africa to India, from Greece to Mexico:

* **from *scaling up* to *scaling across*** – horizontally moving what works from one locality to another. It arises through flexible adaptation and openness to being informed by other communities (as opposed to reliance on outside experts or protecting ideas in a competitive, fearful spirit);

- **from *power* to *play*** – not depending on leaders to motivate and control people as if no one else has motivation or inspiration. 'Play not power evokes people's passion, creativity, and motivation to work hard on seemingly overwhelming challenges' (p. 8);
- **from *problem* to *place*** – instead of large-scale problem-solving by experts, complex issues need to be addressed to create change in education, public safety, art, ecology and food – where people live, on the principle *start anywhere, follow it everywhere*;
- **from *efficiency* to *resilience*** – rather than austerely cutting budgets and staff and resources, notice situations where resilience is being achieved as total systems collapse. '[A] different approach is to engage in a wide range of small local actions that give them the capacity to continuously adapt to an unpredictable and chaotic world' (p. 8);
- **from *transacting* to *gifting*** – instead of a culture promoting the self-interest of the few and scarcity for many, in a gift culture, generosity prevails and there is a growing sense that people have all that they need;
- **from *intervention* to *friendship*** – instead of being disempowered by reliance on experts from elsewhere, local communities grow through learning to trust the capacities and creativity to address their needs, generated by friendship;
- **from *hero* to *host*** – when a community abandons the notion that the cavalry will be coming or that a hero will rescue them from impossible dilemmas, it is released into operating through 'conversational processes to address complex problems, such as health care, homelessness, poverty, and more' (p. 9).

Small groups of people trusting each other in vulnerability and dedication develop strength, stamina and motivation.

An example of the turn to intimacy in expanding notions of Christian community and institutions would include the emphasis on hospitality as a key to mission and ministry. Sheryl A. Kujawa-Holbrook (Professor of Practical Theology and Religious Education at the Methodist Claremont School of Theology in Southern California) and Fredrica Harris Thompsett (Emeritus Professor of Historical Theology in the Anglican Episcopal Divinity School, Cambridge, Massachusetts) write of transformation as a journey, a process for congregational engagement rather than a destination, and its uniqueness to every context. While they see no precise formula for intentional hospitality, they list characteristics that suggest a congregation's movement towards engagement with an extensive and intentional spirit of hospitality:

- **community identity** clearly formed and commitment to a vision of inclusivity and community outreach;
- **openness to marginalized persons** and those not traditionally served by organized religion;
- **worship and ritual that is indigenous** and communicates and supports the congregation's mission and ministry, while at the same time being flexible enough to allow for guests to participate fully, to the degree they choose;
- **all-age spiritual formation and religious education** that supports individuals spiritually and in vocation and witness in the world;
- **community orientated** emergent ministries that are focused on the needs of the wider neighbourhood and planned and undertaken in partnership with those served;
- **collaborative leadership** willing to take risks and undertake projects with uncertain outcomes;
- **authentic leaders** who preach and teach about the integral nature of hospitality for Christian community and who model their commitment to the same;
- *of* not *for* **people:** a perspective of the congregation as the source of *both* spiritual formation *and* transformation of its members in the midst of constant change – these congregations see change as an opportunity and new relationships as a gift;
- **a spirit of generosity:** the willingness to devote the congregation's gifts and resources – human, money, property – to the mission of the wider neighbourhood served;
- **always discerning:** the ability to re-engage and reinterpret ancient truths in the contemporary context; in other words, theology that is emergent and fluid rather than fixed and static, in an atmosphere that allows for questions and challenges.

(adapted with thanks from Kujawa-Holbrook and Thompsett 2010, p. 47)

In similar vein, in questions on the language of worship, Ruth C. Duck (Associate Professor of Worship at Garrett-Evangelical Theological Seminary, Evanston, Illinois) and Patricia Wilson-Kastner (late priest, writer and educator) contribute to our understanding of God as a living, self-revealing reality. They emphasize the importance of churches expressing and making present the experience of encounters with God in mutual relationships:

> we need an expanded language about God that encompasses the experience of women in their God-given humanity and strengthens and empowers their liberation and their growth in the 'image and likeness of God' in which, as Genesis assures us, God created us all.
>
> (Duck and Wilson-Kastner 1999, p. 20)

And I would add that, as Fr Richard Rohr and others remind us, for men there is also the journey to renew language and church culture today; to know they are God's beloved in partnership rather than inherited patterns of dominance. In their epilogue, Duck and Wilson-Kastner offer many practical experiments with language and liturgies to reinforce the sense of 'the Lord is here!'

The sense of God present in our deepest selves is articulated by the psychotherapist Brian Thorne. The core conditions of his work have been acceptance, empathy and congruence. In *Person-Centred Counselling* he describes his experience as a child of 'a mystical encounter which endowed me with a deep sense of my own unique worth and of my essential lovableness' (1991, p. vii). This encounter with the living Jesus triggered by witnessing a church outdoor procession on Good Friday 1946 determined his future life's work, rooted in an 'unshakable conviction that love is the primary force in the universe no matter how great the evidence may be to the contrary' (p. 19). His work arises from surrender to what is in the moment:

> It is this mystery that both sustains and challenges me in my work as a Therapist. On the one hand, it provides me with the assurance that, on those occasions when my client and I feel most stuck, there are resources readily available to us if only we can trust each other enough to allow them access. On the other hand, it challenges me to be in a way that mutual trust of this awesome magnitude can be established between us. Nothing could further be removed from the role of the

objective clinician. Instead I am required to be transparent and vulnerable as I surrender to the process of what I have come to recognize as disciplined intimacy. (p. ix)

Space does not permit more than a mention of the work of the progressive educationalists John Dewey and Parker Palmer, the pedagogy of Paolo Freire or the visionary practice in the L'Arche Communities founded by Jean Vanier. As a final illustration of the urgency to work from presence and immediacy, I turn to the prominent Anglican theologian Mark McIntosh (formerly Van Mildert Professor of Divinity at Durham University). In *Divine Teaching* he asks why was the experience of God as almost overwhelming giver of abundance, beyond all human expectations, so important to Jesus? It was the encounter with this intense blessing from God that Jesus embodied within the frailty of the human condition. This is what made possible the healing, transformation and reconciliation in those who experienced Jesus' face-to-face invitation, 'follow me'. It was a life he knew as flowing to him without reserve through the Spirit, from the Father (2008, pp. 117–18). Jesus himself came to be recognized as the very incarnation of this life to be communicated to others who could also come to share in it.

He prepares people for this sharing in divine life through acts of hospitality, generosity, mercy and forgiveness finally focused in crucifixion and by his sending the Spirit of this life to his disciples that they might do greater works (John 14.12). In his baptism in John's renewal movement, Jesus stands among people, sharing in their expectation of God's salvation (Mark 1.9–11):

> The grace, the loving abundance that Jesus knows as the very root of his being – and which radiates into the world definitively as the resurrection of Jesus from the dead – is the expression in our world of an infinite giving, the free self-sharing of the Father to the Son and in the Spirit or what Christians call the Trinity. (McIntosh 2008, pp. 117–18)

In his ministry, Jesus healed and restored people to the dignity of life in its fullness. This was not through theories *about* God but through giving to others the same encounter he knew with the God he dared to address in intimate relationship – as a son to his father. His disciples witnessed his intimate conversations with God whom he called 'Abba'. His life, death and resurrection open a way for us to have a new standing before and in God. He rocked the religious establishment by presuming to speak, heal and restore people to relationship as one from and one with God the Father.

Our ways of being Church are pregnant with the New Testament experiences of the earliest disciples. Added to this are our own personal and communal glimpses of transformation through God's love. The accumulation of the Holy Spirit given to us in baptism, the witness of many others and the persistent calling of the Trinitarian God empower us to be agents of drawing the world into the patterns of God's own life.

Can conversation transform churches?

A deep undercurrent of this book is that churches must learn to trust their own inner authority, emotions and the peace that comes from encountering God (see Matthew 9.22; Mark 5.34; Luke 7.50 and 8.48). There can be anxiety that keeps some away from group conversation. Some are nervous of saying the 'wrong' thing or exposing their doubts. Others are nervous of being overwhelmed by the apparent certainty of others or by sharing feelings. But we all need the assurance – especially if our life experience has previously been negative – that intimate conversation is not a trap or a route to punishment. An important mantra is that 'No one believes it all and no one believes it all the time.' Christian tradition is a never-ending and broad river in which the experiences, hearts and minds of artists, musicians and worshippers take their part with Scripture and the long centuries of practice and mistakes in many situations. We are contemporary pilgrims on this trail and can make little progress unless we engage bodies and hearts as well as thoughts.

On the evening of the resurrection two very downcast disciples were walking the road home to Emmaus. Without recognizing him, they fell in with Jesus, as a travelling companion. Conversation on recent experiences, interwoven with the Scriptures, and his breaking bread together with them, led to a fiery transformation of their hearts. This superabundant blessing from God proved too much for them to hold on to. Immediately they took to the road again, to share this new disclosure of God with their friends: 'They told what had happened on the road, and how he had been made known to them in the breaking of the bread' (Luke 24.35).

Over 2,000 years later, Christian churches face the question of whether our hearts burn within us as we walk with Jesus on the road. Positively, many are asking: 'How can we respond to God's call with our whole being, in very new circumstances?' or 'How can Christian congregations increasingly become disciples in mission?' This is highlighted when churches are facing a sudden or relentless death: through lack of faith, of people, of heating; through having too many buildings in the wrong place, or too much furniture that restricts versatility; or through regional ways of doing business that hinder rather than release local church energy. There is the perennial question of 'growth', for which transformational conversations are needing to take place. Here is merely the start of a list of issues:

- In what senses is God wanting this church to 'grow' at this time?
- What forms of worship will most nurture existing Christians and invite the participation of others?
- How can we positively honour the spiritual pathways of one generation while opening doors to many other routes that are developing?
- How do congregations grow in responsibility, moving from dependency on a minister, and recognize ministries as callings to be shared and mutually supported?
- How do we build up the worshipping church – in every sense – while working for the good of the neighbourhood?

Despite the search for renewed energy within local churches, there is the resistant backwash of wider cultural pressures, such as the indifference and suspicion of Western society towards Christian faith. Although the rise of energetic new forms of Church can be an encouragement to traditional patterns of Church, they can also sap their confidence and denude local churches, so threatening their continued existence. Added to this, many churches routinely respond from within the pathos of victimhood. Echoing Old Testament grief at lost glory (Lamentations 3.42–43, 49–54; Psalms 55.2–5 and 56.5–6a) there is a sense of innocently receiving an unjust sentence: 'What have we done to deserve this? There is nothing we can do.'

The woman in Mark's narrative (Mark 5.21–43) is not only healed personally, but through telling her story before Jesus and those around her is restored by Jesus to her community. Weaving together these two strands, this book invites the discovery of a church's *present* response to God's gifts now. Out of God's deep blessing, how can a church increase its capacity as a self-giving agent of God's own mission in the world? Through choosing to be a blessing (however ridiculous that may seem), how do Christian communities grow in their at-one-ness with God? I shall explore how encountering, listening deeply and respecting one another in conversation can transform community energy and potential. There is of course traction in discussion and debate to understand and accept the elements that compose current dilemmas, but here I want to explore the generative potential of conversation, sharing experiences, dreams, feelings, peace and well-being.

Stephen Pickard, at an international gathering of ministry developers in Texas in 2015, spoke informally of 'slow church'. He was suggesting that instead of rushing headlong into innovative measures to shore up the old church, we could become active contemplatives for whom the absolute assurance of living in blessing, in the utter reliability of God, is always a priority. There seem to me to be so many resonances with this in Scripture, such as the long journey of Moses and God's people from Egypt to the Promised Land or the time spent by Jesus in the desert at the start of his public ministry. We can trace this in the disciplines of ethnography (see the close studies of local communities by Timothy Jenkins, 1999) and in what experts in literature call a methodical 'close reading' of texts (see, for example, University of Warwick, <www2.warwick.ac.uk/fac/arts/english/currentstudents/undergraduate/modules/fulllist/second/en227/closereading>). In theology, Daniel W. Hardy became passionate about the pilgrimage, what he described as the 'pre-estimated' walking of Jesus around Galilee (Hardy, Ford and Ochs 2010, pp. 24–39). Completing this book just a few yards from the Leeds–Liverpool Ship Canal, I am constantly aware of the passage of unique and colourful boats. Families and groups constantly progressing, talking and sharing food and drink, at walking speed, remind me of the slow time required to curate a communal space in which to explore deep questions with renewed energy, insight and hope. Luke's story of the Emmaus Road journey (Luke 24.13–35) is an invitation for friends to talk together on the way, often not recognizing immediately who it is that accompanies them. The outcome of hearts on fire together is, I believe, one of the greatest blessings God has to offer us today.

In summary, the approach to the renewal of churches I am advocating is rooted in the spirit of Beatitude:

- Jesus' invitation for churches to move from ways of isolation and antagonism
- openness to abundance and deepening communion with the Trinitarian God
- movement within God's way of overflowing blessing, as shown in Jesus.

PART 1

A CONVERSATIONAL PATHWAY FOR CHANGING CHURCHES

1 Sharing God's blessing

The loving abundance that Jesus knows as the very root of his being is the expression in our world of an eternal abundance . . . the free self-sharing of the Father to the Son in the Spirit.

(McIntosh 2008, p. 118)

Churches blessed through blessing others

As part of an emerging and unfinished international ecumenical conversation, this book is a resource for:

- **stimulating** churches to recognize at the heart of Christian faith the invitation of God in the present moment, for groups of Christians to know themselves as 'beloved' and as 'friends', sharing joyfully in the relationship of Jesus and his Father (Abba). My passion is that this will release for many others the blessing of knowing and living in the abundant, reconciling, self-giving life that Jesus shows and makes possible.
- **inviting** churches to become part of an interdisciplinary movement that evokes appreciative and conversational attitudes and skills, and so to engage with many fields of thinking and action, through:

  - **looking for** and listening to new signs of life or changes in the use of language, growing in empathy, paying attention to others, having a creative approach to difference;
  - **encouraging** positive responses, celebrating fruitful developments, growing in self-awareness and self-appreciation, asking searching questions and listening to the answers;
  - **going beyond** formal, ritualized ways of relating to being more *present* to God, others, society and to ourselves, creating healthy institutions that remain respectful of all participants in conflicted situations, living with complexity and being watchful when we are drawn to be dominating or controlling;

- **encouraging** the creation and affirmation of conversation through networks of the ministry of companionship, willing and capable of building trust in local churches seeking to respond again to God's mission in the world.

Mutual appreciation

The expectation of being blessed and of being a blessing is a deep wisdom within Scripture. Christians believe that Jesus showed how we can come to stand in the same place as himself – in relation to God the Father through the Spirit. We can experience loving protection, we can be drawn out in a fiery inspiration, we can lay down our own will in obedience, we can come to know our truest self and purpose in life and we can be brought to a final point of utter fullness, beatitude.

The conversations I am describing and advocating in this book do not deny the need for churches to debate, discuss and disagree about matters of Christian identity and practice. In a world that acknowledges complexity and a Church rooted in Trinitarian relationality, I am navigating a way beyond mere binary opposites. In order to step beyond an adversarial approach to discerning the future, sometimes we need to sit together as equals and listen carefully as each of us speaks from our considerable experience. Sometimes we need to make space to speak and be heard and express our deepest feelings without censure or interruption, just as we are, without the pressure to meet an ideal level of faith or goodness.

Living out of abundance

Churches are communities that trust they have been given the gift of what Paul calls 'a new creation' (2 Cor. 5.17), 'springing from something utterly mysterious, taking place in the interplay between Jesus, the One he called "abba" and the Spirit, an interaction definitively expressed in Jesus' death and resurrection' (McIntosh 2008, p. 114).

To know we are blessed that we might become a blessing; to know that in blessing others we ourselves are blessed – these are God-given ways of calling us as Church into a renewed identity. Blessing is not a fixed thing or a possession given rigidly, from one to another. Rather it is an energizing movement of God in and towards all creation, which we experience and seek to give expression to.

Jesus showed and embodied a life of blessing through intense engagement with God, whom he called 'Father', and a full and messy engagement with raw and damaged aspects of life. Through Jesus, early Christians came to recognize in God a unity that is at the same time a constantly shifting flow of relating between the three persons of Father, Son and Spirit. Eventually early Christians came to give the name 'Trinity' to their encounter with God.

The search continues in every age to put into words experience of God as relational, a ceaseless outflow and return, constantly making, sustaining, inviting, loving, drawing close to and keeping all things and all people. Some have suggested that in our breathing in and out, all living beings are praising the Lord – in the aspiration of the Hebrew (Old Testament) name for God, *Yah . . . weh.*

One of the challenges for churches is that our operational theology of God and God's ways with the world bear little connection with such Trinitarian experiences or concepts. This has a direct effect on how we conceive and practise everything Christian. So inherited patterns of worship largely portray blessing as a single movement from the ordained towards everyone else. In that way the act of blessing reinforces a solo and patriarchal expression of religious authority. We shall explore how an alternative wisdom about blessing arises from recognizing God in constant abundance or overflow towards and among all creation. Passionately, God invites a thankful, repenting and purposeful response to a loving initiative.

At the heart of all reality, in a spiralling dynamic, God blesses creation; creation blesses God; God blesses humanity; humanity blesses God; creation blesses humanity; humanity blesses creation; we bless one another – and so it continues. Perhaps the image of a helix column or a twisted spiral cord best illustrate this notion – the DNA of love.

Some ask whether we can really bless God. Surely we are too sinful and it all works the other way around. But blessing God is not conferring on God what God does not have already, except our response as God's beloved. In praising God we are recognizing how we are caught up in a spiral of encounter as 'blessed', and thanking God as the source of all blessing. Also in accepting our blessing as a gift held in trust, we are lured by God into being advance signs and agents of final beatitude of the whole creation.

Recognizing holiness

In families, towns, villages and churches we come across individuals who, intuitively, we recognize as daughters and sons of God, blessed, beloved ones, sharing God's blessing and unconsciously blessing others, with little self-regard. Characters from Scripture can help us to recognize some of the traits of blessedness. Like Jesus they can encourage us to step into our own calling as blessed and as beloved communities. When we are blessed liturgically, it is significantly in the form of a cross. Anyone in Scripture blessed into commissioned roles and tasks travelled an uncertain and costly road in the company of the Trinitarian God who suffered with them:

- **Moses** – who encountered God in the bush that was burning but not consumed, was commissioned to lead his people out of injustice.
- **Elizabeth** – mother of John the forerunner, pronounces to Mary, pregnant with Jesus, how she will be remembered for all time as a blessing.
- **Mary** – in turn blesses the God who is a blessing to the poor who are raised up in new dignity.
- **Jesus** – blesses the disciples and departs from them; joyfully they bless God in the temple and later bless others through the life of the baptized communities given life as the corporate risen Lord.
- **Paul** – the highly placed Pharisee who dramatically loses his sight as he recognizes God truly in Jesus; embraced by followers of the risen Christ, he becomes an agent of blessing in small new churches around the Mediterranean.

Go ahead – be a blessing!

One of the key insights into blessing in the New Testament is given to us by Matthew's Gospel (5.1–12), commonly known as the Beatitudes. The Palestinian Christian, Elias Chacour, suggests that a knowledge of Aramaic, the language of Jesus, can enrich our understanding of

Jesus' core message. He believes we are not merely to consider ourselves as objects of blessing, following the Greek *Makarioi*. Looking further back to the Aramaic, the word Jesus may have used is *Ashray* (from the verb *Yashar*). This is far from a passive connotation. Instead it means 'to set yourself on the right way for the right goal; to turn around, repent; to become straight or righteous'. Chacour explains:

> When I understand Jesus' words in the Aramaic, I translate like this: 'Get up, go ahead, do something, move, you who are hungry and thirsty for justice, for you shall be satisfied. Get up, go ahead, do something, move, you peacemakers, for you shall be called children of God.' To me this reflects Jesus' words and teachings, much more accurately. I can hear him saying, 'Get your hands dirty to build a human society for human beings; otherwise others will torture and murder the poor, the voiceless and the powerless.' Christianity is not passive but active, energetic, alive, going beyond despair. (Chacour 2001, p. 144)

Blessed in the mess

Christian wisdom grows through struggle in chaos rather than by keeping ourselves secure. Churches exist to form us in Christ for the world's sake. Being Church together is God's way of helping us be as fully open as we dare to expanding possibilities of healing and to grasp new opportunities for unity, compassion and love. God's blessing – 'speaking well of' – initiates life, always in the freedom and respect God has for creation. We are perfectly at liberty to disregard a blessing and live with the consequences for ourselves and others. Here is our inherent sinful tendency not to believe in God's loving us despite all our refusals and breaking of vows.

Some will protest that this approach of focusing on God's desire to draw humanity communally and personally towards authenticity and joy ignores the evil of the world ('original sin'). The Benedictine monk David Steindl-Rast, recognizing human sinfulness as 'something wrong with existence', coins the phrase 'Human life grinds on its axle'. 'Not only the Buddhist and Christian but every religious tradition starts from the recognition that we are disordered, lost and seeking our way home' (in Capra et al. 1991, p. 41). With today's media coverage of so much that degrades, shames and degenerates human living, it is inevitably tempting to numb ourselves with distractions, seek ways of propping up our self-interest and even seek spiritual paths of innocent solitude and calm. The scriptural wisdom tradition recognizes within the complexities and deep fragmentation of living the unfailing presence, forgiveness and love of God. The psalms especially remind us that God may often despair of us and yet never gives up; equally, we may sometimes be so angry with God that we are tempted to hide or walk away. But letting God be God, never fully comprehensible to us, can only lead us to the security of living by trust in the one from whom all blessings flow, proclaiming 'Blessed be God for ever'.

Genesis 1 describes the origin of creation through God's presence within the seething turbulence of the deep, when the earth was as yet a formless void (Keller 2003). Consistent with God's powerful presence in vulnerability, Jesus immerses himself in human life for the healing of those trapped in sickness of every kind (see Phil. 2.6–8). He adds no further shame to what they and others have already brought on themselves.

The New Testament letter to Christians in Ephesus contains many encouraging messages for churches in every age. One of its themes is of Church as the mystery of God's age-old wisdom shown in Christ. The very real practical anxieties of churches in troubled times are lifted into another horizon.

The mess and provisionality of the churches we are part of are also constantly regenerated within the infinite, unending expansiveness of God's desire to help bring creation to its fulfilment. God is constantly creating the event we call 'church' for the sake of the world's completion. Our participation is possible and blessed because of God's constant movement towards us and towards everything. Mark McIntosh, interpreting Paul in 2 Corinthians 5.17 ('if anyone is in Christ, there is a new creation'), insists on God's unconditional love and reliability:

> There is a very real way in which God's knowing and cherishing God's idea of each creature is what safeguards each creature's freedom and its true identity. No matter what befalls it, no matter what lies about itself it may be told, its authentic goodness and identity are still alive in God, and may by grace (and ultimately by resurrection) be restored to the creature . . . in which everything has been made new.
>
> (2008, p. 209)

When we meet and speak truthfully in church conversations it is through this original and transformative energy of God. This gives us the capacity to go beyond our natural strength and judgements. Although sharing more of ourselves in group processes can seem difficult and unpleasant, the presence of the God of Jesus can keep us going until we feel braver.

> And it's right here in the dirt,
> where we've both been loved and hurt,
> that love himself has come to pitch his tent.
>
> ('Angels Unawares', in Guite 2013)

2 Participatory and appreciative inquiry

We become part of the transformation we hope for as our imaginations
are resourced by the Spirit, and in our transformation we draw forward
and transform the reality around us.

(Quash 2013, p. 279)

Between 2013 and 2015 my research fellowship opened up opportunities to spend time with groups of various sizes within local churches,
mainly but not entirely within the North-East of England. When a
university-based researcher invites himself to a church, people could
be forgiven for fearing the worst: that they will be observed, measured,
compared, counted, objectified, categorized, analysed, recorded and
published. Instead, my intention in setting out on this research was
to walk with small church communities that were experiencing what
is common now in mainline churches: a sense of the tide having gone
out, leaving them stranded. They have certain speech-act patterns
inherited from a previous era, patterns that still can bring comfort to
participants but are alien and bewildering to others. Even more anxiety-
creating is the not to be voiced fear that this faith may no longer be
'true' in that it seems to lack connection with rationality, common
sense and a society of compulsion and mutual exploitation. Although
my intention was to build on my previously acquired consultation
skills through working with participatory and appreciative-inquiry
approaches, my deepest desire was to stimulate and encourage churches
to know and share God's blessing – as shown in Jesus and made present through God's Spirit.

Core theological assumptions: Church, Christ
and revelation

A core assumption in my theological approach is that the mission and
life of the Christian community in society is best informed by drawing on a range of human disciplines. That is not the same as Christian

theology capitulating to so-called secular theories but is rather the attempt to discern God's presence in all of life. So in this book I have explored my leading theological themes with the benefit of a Participatory Action Research (PAR) approach. This has given a grammar to my long-held intuition that theology, and theories of the practical management of organizations, are potentially complementary resources. The literature in this field is vast and expanding, with slight variations in language. One of my particular sources has been the framework of ideas and practices called Action Inquiry, developed by Bill Torbert and his associates Dal Fischer and David Rooke. They make clear the value of becoming consciously aware, moment-to-moment, of the effectiveness, validity and legitimacy of our interpersonal relations as we attempt to negotiate and collaborate with one another in purposeful activity. Practitioners of PAR work from the basis that in a healthily functioning organization, every person involved will be fully attentive to the whole. This requires a congruence between espoused purpose, strategy, operations and outcomes. So when everyone pays attention to everything what emerges is the "true natural sanity of awareness of the whole"' (Torbert 1991, p. 291).

One of the key benefits of a PAR perspective is to encourage practitioners to observe and map our own learning journey and to notice the influence of many relationships we have with colleagues close at hand, as well as with those known through the inspiration of their writing. As a long-term committed reflective practitioner, I am glad to recognize that my earliest inspiration as a parish priest in the second half of the twentieth century sprang from the insights of Vatican II, the World Council of Churches Lima texts on Baptism, Eucharist and Ministry and the explosion of practice stimulated by the writings of Hans Küng, Edward Schillebeeckx, Jürgen Moltmann, Leonardo Boff, Enrique Dussel, the critical educationalist Paulo Freire and pioneers of basic Christian community in South America, Minjung Theology in Korea, Black Theology and Feminist Theology.

In the introduction to a World Council of Churches publication on doing theology in community, *Theology by the People*, edited by Samuel Amirtham and John S. Pobee, is a prayer that closes with the demand for a blessing:

Will you then not be with us, God?
Will you then not wrestle with us here in this place?
For we will not let you go until you bless us.
Gloria a tí Senor, Gloria a tí
En el nombre del Padre, del Hijo y del Espiritu Santo,
Amen.
(A. L. de García, in Amirtham and Pobee 1986, p. vii)

A core value of a participatory approach to being Church and of the learning associated with that is that all can find there the liberation and dignity that characterizes membership of the body of Christ. This involves finding ways of dismantling – literally 'uncloaking' or 'defortifying' – forms of church authority and learning that subdue, silence and inhibit, rather than release energy, imagination and multi-vocal creativity. However, before I say a word about fostering vulnerable churches, I have to have the conversation with myself and God: 'What is there for me as a person as well as an ecclesiologist that God longs for me to dismantle?' The completely different way of seeing everything that comes, notably in the works of Jean Vanier, is a challenging reminder to practitioners not to escape into abstractions, dreams and theories that bypass real relating. There can be no true renewal of churches till leaders and prophets let God break open our own defensive games.

An image that resonates with me is that of a tree with strong roots that destabilize the walls of buildings and push their way through cracks in the fabric. My theological assumptions about ecclesiology, Christology and revelation continue to be that:

- Disciples of Christ are formed together in their difference through engagement with the intense holiness of God, experienced as the rhythm of outgoing and return of loving energy in the whole of creation.
- Church is primarily and essentially communal, a people called into being by God's word and the sacraments (1 Peter 2.9–10; Matt. 18.20; Rom. 12.5).
- Each baptized Christian and baptizing Christian community is given gifts to share responsibility for making Christ known and to be a light for the world (Isa. 42.6).

- Directly every Christian can share in the life of the risen Christ through God's Spirit (1 Tim. 2.5; Heb. 8.6; 9.15; 12.24).
- Clergy and leaders bear vital and particular responsibility for helping Christian people to be Church in various ways, but must never themselves simply be equated with the community of love (1 Cor. 12.11; 2 Pet. 1.1). *All* as they are able moment by moment are called essentially as missional disciples.
- In the light of God's word, churches attend fully to the world's agendas and offer prophetic and critical engagement with society and the created world. 'It is a church of the people, with the values of the people, with their language, liturgical expressions and popular religiosity' (Boff 1985, p. 34).
- Clergy have often been set up from every direction to 'police' popular religious feeling that does not conform to official belief. Yet who does not know the wide range of religious ideas within a single congregation? Belief that works in real life has to be forged in the experience and struggles of people through illness, brokenness and combating injustice, as well as in times of peace, joy and fulfilment. In this chaordic movement, never standing still but in constant flux, is the detailed context within which Christians take part in God's mission and ministry.
- The people of God do theology together against the background of Jesus Christ, God's servant accepting humiliation and crucifixion to show the meaning of love. God's beloved are invited to enter that same relationship of intimacy that Jesus shared with God whom, shockingly, he dared address as 'Abba' (Gal. 4.6–7; Rom. 8.14–15).
- Matthew shows God revealed in the hungry, the thirsty, the naked, the stranger and the imprisoned (25.31–46). Theology and growth in self-understanding belongs to 'merest children', everyone in local communities of all kinds (11.25). When we pray *our* Father, we admit our being joined to and responsible for our neighbour, locally and globally.
- We receive our knowledge of and call from God in Scripture and all are able to enter into conversation arising from the text. But the daily experiences of people, families, churches and societies are also the grist in which God's desire for relationship and work of

healing is revealed. Scripture and experience belong together and are not rivals.

- So the formation of God's people through processes of learning and transformation is to equip disciples to read and respond to their context in the light of the core values of the gospel. The heart of the Christian learning advocated in this book can be summarized in these two statements:

> Theological education is theological in the sense that it involves people in a commitment to mission and ministry, a commitment to the 'study of God' in the sense of his revelation in the life, death and resurrection of Jesus Christ and his continuous working through the Holy Spirit.
>
> (H. M. Zorn, in Amirtham and Pobee 1986, p. 17)

- And, drawing out pointers for the future of theological thinking:

> Dan ... in his conversation with me is taking for granted what may be called a deep grammar: a constant interplay between the Bible doctrines and a range of contemporary questions and discourses. At its simplest this suggests a basic condition for fruitful, educated, theological thinking: competence in understanding Scripture, the doctrines and a range of current disciples.
>
> (Ford, in Hardy, Ford and Ochs 2010, p. 130)

Appreciative Inquiry

This book offers a mere introduction to Appreciative Inquiry (AI), a conversation-based approach to organizational change. It arises within conversation about the nature of power as relational and learning as holistic, and recognizes the potency of emotional energy to bring about change. Advocates of AI methodology would say that it changes the way we talk, relate and give dignity to every participant. The key is its conversation-based blending of theory, practice and life experience.

The chartered occupational psychologist Sarah Lewis and colleagues advocate AI methodology for its attention to context and adaptability to the needs of those involved and the time realistically available. They describe the practice as recognizable:

as people meet and talk together . . . So although the event concludes with the production of an action plan, that is not to say that nothing has happened until this point. The new relationships people have formed during their experience of the event, and the different experiences they have had, are of themselves an important change in their experience of the organization. The stories they have told that hadn't been told before, the dreams they have created of the future, and the ideas they have developed of how things can be and what needs to be done have all acted to change their experience of the world and so have effectively changed the world. The energy generated by the event is supported by the action plans; it is not a product of it.   (Lewis et al. 2008, p. 55)

This discipline seems highly appropriate for churches to engage with in a time of anxiety and negativity. It nudges them into acquiring the attitude and skills to challenge stories of unmitigated misery. An alarm bell might ring if it were thought that to encourage an AI way of reframing churches allowed no room for facing negatives. There are undoubtedly multiple systemic faults in how we are Church, for example in the ways churches too frequently fail to nurture Christian practice and spirituality, discern and nurture vocations and make and support leadership appointments. It would be naïve to ignore these sustained faults, indifferent to the pain that churches as institutions cause to many. These require rigorous critique. But this is not the same as losing energy through the dominance of a persistent despondency and pathos. Churches are called to live from the story of a very particular and unpredictable God who in a costly way has interrupted our preferred narratives.

No one expresses this more convincingly, in my view, than the biblical theologian Walter Brueggemann when he insists churches submit to a different rhetoric from *business as usual*. In his rereading of the text of the Philistines taking to their temple the Ark of the Covenant (1 Sam. 4—6), he reveals the character of the Lord (*YHWH* in Hebrew) as one who breaks despair:

At the nadir of the night the true character of YHWH acts towards home and will not be held. It is this self-starting God who has always been the ground of hope for the church in its despair . . . This narrative about the self-starting God who breaks the powers of the night, does not depend on Israelite hands to defeat Dagon; it has moreover no interest in the restoration of what is old and cherished and failed. This God never looks back, but moves in a flamboyant way to newness.

(Brueggemann 2002, p. 51)

AI describes the methodology of seeking lasting change from eight principles:

1 **Words create worlds** – our common life is created through the words we use and how we talk to one another.
2 **Inquiry creates change** – asking questions is the start of a change.
3 **We can choose what we study** – what we choose to look at, from all the possibilities, makes the world as we know it.
4 **Image inspires action** – our image of the future shapes our present daily actions.
5 **Positive questions lead to positive change** – to change a culture requires positive questions asked by hopeful groups and teams.
6 **Wholeness brings out the best** – when everyone comes together in conversation, creativity and capacity are generated.
7 **Acting *as if* is self-fulfilling** – to innovate for the future we desire, we have to become the change.
8 **Free choice liberates power** – when people are involved in making organizational choices, commitment, excellent practice and positive change emerge.

AI creates a culture of:

• **Discovering** – appreciating what is and what has been for the community and individuals.
• **Conceiving** – imagining what might be through working together boldly and purposefully.
• **Designing** – giving shape to pictures of the future.
• **Improvising** – learning together how things could be and what leadership will be required.

As a way of furthering progress towards becoming an adult Christian community, AI distinctively offers churches a resource for creating emerging and unfinished conversation, as a distinctive ethos. The use of AI, patiently over time, along with existing Christian disciplines –

such as biblical study, liturgy, hospitality and contemplation – forms a community in conversation-based practice.

- AI can transform groups from being meetings of individuals into 'spaces' that are free and alive.
- AI helps groups to grow in courage and discover a creative flow that can amaze, surprise and take us beyond what we would think possible.
- AI can help overcome anxiety about approaching change.
- AI creates groups where we can be known, heard, dream, take part, try something new and be positive.
- AI recognizes the best in people and the world around us, finds those things that give health, aliveness and joy, affirms past and present strengths, gifts and potential and builds capacity in churches.
- AI makes space for us to ask questions, investigate and to explore what matters to us now.
- Through practising AI we learn to ask affirming questions on the topic the group is exploring for the benefit of churches.
- AI draws mutual appreciation together with the search for next steps. It fosters a way of being Church that moves away from top-down hierarchy to a place of shared knowledge and self-organizing processes.

AI has the potential to affirm that a church, in all its membership, embodies enough commitment and resource for positive change to come about.

Asking appreciative questions

The thread that runs through the conversations to which I have been companion is that of inquiring with one another into what makes for this particular church to become more holistic, God-centred and instrumental for the health of the neighbourhood. I have introduced the notion of 'companion' in preference to facilitator, and I will expand on this in Chapter 4. The potential of conversational change relies on groups learning to ask life-giving questions. One of the roles of the companion – though we all need to evaluate ourselves – is to encourage everyone to avoid negative questions or suggestions disguised as questions.

Deliberately in order to follow Jesus' invitation to communion with God and one another, and bypassing setting up sterile adversarial polarities, I am avoiding the word 'discussion', with its Latin roots in 'cutting your opponent to pieces'. Another way of putting this is to seek to be Church assuming that everyone has a voice and the community is richer for living with paradox as a new framing of comprehensiveness (see Robinson 2008, pp. 4–5). AI methodology invites conversations that are curious, supportive and interconnecting. It requires that we are purposively *present* to one another. When I sit down now with groups to ask where God is at work and how God's blessings are known, I often find a release of laughter, tears, the expression of feelings and new energy.

Appreciative questioning generates more and more possibilities, such as:

- Can you say more about a particular time when you really felt valued as part of this team or church?
- Recall a time when you worked well with someone else so that together you made a difference.
- When was a time that you felt at your best here?
- Think of an occasion when your particular skills were fully used.
- What is there about belonging to church here that you feel passionate about?
- When have you not felt blessed or appreciated?

All kinds of productive questions can flow positively from such beginnings:

- What resources did you need?
- Who worked with you?
- What difference did it make?
- How have you dealt with times when you felt alone or unwanted?
- Can you describe what it was like?
- What feelings do you associate with that event or time?

I've witnessed the unexpected possibilities that emerge in meetings of Christian groups of varying size, together with clergy and other leaders. At a convenient time, in a space with an intimate atmosphere, significant conversation can take place. In an informal but carefully structured, agreed period there is the gathering, introductions, prayer,

Scripture, simple input, conversation, shared refreshments, further thoughts, prayer and departure.

Another set of statements and questions I have used to prompt conversation in local church groups are these:

- What is working well?
- What gives cause for dissatisfaction?
- Where is God in your experience of Church now?
- What is your personal commitment/hope?
- Who are you working with?
- What does the word 'blessing' mean in Scripture and the Christian life?
- What do you understand as a 'blessing' in your experience?
- Who do you know who lives in 'blessing'?
- Do you have a sense now of being 'blessed'?
- Who 'blesses' you?
- Whom do you 'bless'?
- How does 'blessing' connect with God as 'Trinity', 'praise' and 'joy' and 'worship'?
- What are you learning about God's 'blessing'?
- How are you deliberately living in God's 'blessing'?
- How is blessing reciprocal?
- How can 'blessing' be a diminishment rather than a liberation?
- How are you/your church ignoring God's 'blessing'?
- What can your church learn from those on the 'edge' or who worship occasionally?

Here are some statements I have found helpful for triggering conversation about the particular role of clergy in local churches:

- Energy leaks from churches when there is a culture of dependence by most people on the few.
- Routinely, congregations make the mistake of expecting clergy and a few 'keen' laity to be overworking superheroes.
- Often clergy become so overwhelmed through taking the weight of maintenance, administration and holding everyone together that there is little energy for review, growth in faith or prayer.
- A reducing proportion of churches believe they have insufficient worshippers and clergy to maintain their inherited patterns. There

is no assumption here as to an ideal size of church or who may or may not exercise ministry or leadership.

- Clergy, despite being fully aware that churches cannot be rescued by overworking leaders, find it painful to see things fail.
- Laity over centuries have not been encouraged to do more than 'help' with what the clergy have no time or energy for.
- The seduction of being the successful omnicompetent cleric still has life in it.
- Discerning the identity of church that will best serve God's mission now requires prayer and deep consideration.
- In a much-quoted poem, 'In Search of a Round Table', Chuck Lathrop contrasts the narrow, long, cross-shaped church with a vision of an encircling, open church, where leaders need to be loved into roundness.

Dynamic conversations on Scripture

AI relates well to experimenting with a dynamic approach to reflecting on Scripture called 'divine reading' (*lectio divina*). This phrase – in Latin! – may seem alarming or unusual. In simplest terms it can be described thus: 'a practice that allows Christians to reclaim a radical simplicity and forge a bond between prayer and life, between spirituality and what is most basic to being human' (Bianchi 2015, p. 18).

Enzo Bianchi, in his study of *lectio divina*, draws out the essentially dialogical nature of Scripture itself so that our reading is always an encounter with God speaking to us in this moment, inviting our response today. Churches have need of all the various disciplines – philological, linguistic, historical, archaeological, literary, comparative – to engage intelligently with texts, but also require that readers and churches allow the Scriptures to speak to the heart in direct, personal and transformative ways. As Psalm 95.7–9 reminds us ('O that today you would listen to his voice!'), each day churches are invited to 'stay alert and encourage one another not to let their hearts harden in sin' (Bianchi 2015, p. 57). An accessible introduction to this increasingly popular 'godly reading', an ancient way of exploring Scripture, is to be found in the Pilgrim Course – <www.pilgrimcourse.org>.

Especially in a group that tells itself it knows little of the Bible, I would:

• present a passage (such as Exod. 14.14; Mark 6.50; John 6.20 or 15.9–11, 15) printed out in a larger than usual font;
• invite people in turn to read a verse;
• hold some silence;
• ask people alone for a moment, and then in twos, to choose a word or phrase that resonates with them;
• invite those who feel able to tell everyone why they chose the words they did.

People have surprised themselves in what they have been moved and empowered to speak out. I have found that the same process works well with many contemporary songs, such as Bernadette Farrell's 'O God, You Search Me', her interpretation of Psalm 139 in which God searches, knows and besieges us.

I would close with a mutual exchange of blessings in which everyone learns a phrase such as 'May the Lord bless you richly' and moves around simply signing others and being signed on the forehead with the mark of the cross. Another way of giving and receiving mutual blessing is to stand in a circle and, without actually touching your neighbour, allow your right hand to reach just over their left hand while everyone in the circle does the same. So everyone's right hand is lifted up and facing palm down while the left hand is down and facing up. Try it! The sense of closeness when you hold that position for at least a minute is very strong.

In my experience these conversations can easily link with one of the pressing questions of any particular church community, such as how to connect with a different strand of people in the neighbourhood, or how to be bolder in managing all-age worship or in planning to admit young ones to receiving Holy Communion. Respectful and yet stretching group experiences such as this have great capacity for helping laity to discover a deep identity as disciples. That seems vital as a prelude to responding to a sense of being called to ministry.

Spending two years walking alongside churches, ecumenically, in the North and North-East of England and in New York, I have learned so much about the resilience and playfulness of small local churches.

Especially I have encountered their desire and capacity for building healthy networks, among themselves and in the neighbourhood and local schools and homes for the elderly. I have also walked with churches experiencing trauma that have emerged stronger through their intentional reliance on God and on one another. I've also valued clergy and leaders who are secure and respectful enough to embody relational and respectful patterns of working. They build trust and self-reflection among those given to their charge.

Bringing them all together

As we connect with others and discover solutions to our problems, our small local efforts can emerge into large-scale change. And then we have the satisfaction of no longer feeling strange or labeled as foolish dreamers, mavericks and crackpots. Our pioneering methods become accepted, normal even, just the way things get done round here.

(Wheatley and Frieze 2011, pp. 46–7)

An illustration of transformation through cooperation and participation was a day hosted by Brunswick Methodist Church in the centre of Newcastle upon Tyne. Facilitated by myself and three practical theologians, Malcolm Grundy, Pat Moran and Diane Westmorland, the gathering was constituted of representatives from Anglican, Methodist and Roman Catholic churches. They had all spent a year experimenting with me in conversations inspired by AI methodology and by my own experience of drawing groups into conversation through humour, hospitality and the growing desire to intensify their life with God and to extend their share in God's mission in their locality.

The primary purpose of bringing them all together was for different groups to take time, slowly making space to share food, hear and receive stories, ideas and practices from one another. The day was designed as an exercise in community development that carefully avoided traditional controlling behaviour by leaders or participants. Specifically our aim was to create a learning space, a gathering of people from various localities to stimulate purposeful energy for the renewing of their churches. The culture of the event was influenced by the organizational theorist Margaret Wheatley. She has coined the phrase 'scaling across' as shorthand for 'releasing knowledge, practices and resources and allowing them to circulate freely so that others may adapt them to their local environment' (Wheatley and Frieze 2011, p. 32).

The main methodology of the day was to promote group conversation at tables. Those who hosted the groups – a mixture of each of the churches represented – encouraged the harvesting of their reactions to conversations I had been leading in their churches. The following questions were given as conversation prompts:

- What was it like to be part of these Conversations of Hope?
- What was helpful to your church and to you personally?
- What emerged as a result?

Below is a representative sample of responses:

- We are becoming more outward-looking.
- More people are coming to our church and we are reaching out more to others.
- Our people feel more enthusiastic.
- Doing this has helped us to share our faith stories.
- We are building things for others to use in the future.
- I have become less judgemental and more able to see God in others.
- We have been learning to see how much God blesses us.
- We're feeling invigorated, encouraging what was already there but we didn't see it.
- We are becoming more self-aware – and aware of each other.
- People are opening up and talking more about their faith.
- I appreciate more what God is doing in my life.
- We are going forward with Christ.
- The conversations have been non-threatening.
- We communicate better now.
- We are becoming more proactive in ministry.
- I'm looking forward to what will come next!

David, a Roman Catholic priest, summed up his experience of the conversations as churches face grave challenges about diminishing congregations, a shortage of vocations to priesthood and many associated factors:

I get the sense that we are being drawn, almost pushed, by God and pulled by the environment and circumstances we're swimming in. We have to let go of all our agendas and plans which no longer work. We are to search, by listening, by being still and allowing God to speak to us, through what mainstream churches are now facing.

Our collective 'not-knowing', not being in control is helping us to rely on God who is leading us, but in the dark. That is the current 'blessing', though it doesn't feel or look like it. Just as Jesus wasn't the Messiah people expected. A deep impression that came to me at the gathering was that we're on a wilderness journey, a new Exodus from what is familiar and causing us pain. Or we're like those disciples at Easter and before Pentecost, unsure what to do next. If that's true, then the present journey will give birth to a deeper faith and resilient life together, an 'emerging church', as some have described it, a communion of diversity, radiating the nature of God.

Participatory Action Research

I share the view that the perspective and attitude of the research process need to be of the same character as the intention to offer ways for local communities to discover more freedom to be what God is calling them to be. It has been immensely encouraging to discover the international movement that comes under several names but which many describe as Participatory Action Research (PAR). This perspective works from a profound respect for all involved in a learning situation. It seeks to draw together action and reflection, theory and practice, in mutual participation, in order to discover practical solutions to issues of vital concern to people and communities. I had a sense that this methodology, moving away from a modernist or positivist approach to facilitation (with the fiction that it's possible to be a detached observer), would support my intuitive holistic and contextual approach to learning and development. Also implicit is the recognition that real transformation comes from genuine participation by everyone, in appropriate ways.

PAR is a research perspective rather than a fixed process. The expression acts like an umbrella, referring to research committed to democratic and inclusive principles so that 'democratically developed knowledge' may contribute actively to socially innovative, collective actions. PAR is characterized by researchers and practitioners joining in promoting democratic and social changes in 'a shared commitment to democratic social change' (Brydon-Miller 2003, p. 8; see also Anderson and Bilfeldt 2012).

PAR seeks to empower people and communities through connecting three aspects of theory and practice, leading to collective action:

1 critical societal diagnosis;
2 democratic knowledge building from the bottom up;
3 the facilitation of processes of long-term social innovation.

I am drawn to the following definition of community-based participatory research (CBPR) by the Centre for Social Justice and Community Action of the University of Durham (<www.durham.ac.uk/beacon/socialjustice>):

> An approach to research based on commitment to sharing power and resources and working towards beneficial outcomes for all participants, especially 'communities' (groups of people who share something in common or groups based on common identity, interest or practice). It may be led and undertaken by members of community groups and organizations themselves, or by community groups working alongside, or in partnership with, professional researchers (including academics and research students).

A self-reflexive approach has been a key strand in subverting the expectation of dependency on authority figures. I had to bring into awareness the temptation in myself and in local church participants to have secret access to a solution to their problems. My intention is more about helping them to take another look, to find a new gaze, a *metanoia*. In Christian terms, Jesus' own temptations to misuse his authority – focused in the 40 days in the desert but never finally dismissed – seemed very pertinent. Similarly, the Feeding of the Five Thousand is a classic reminder for churches not to adopt the myth of scarcity as a way of avoiding sharing in God's mission. Holistic notions of learning identify three modes of facilitation – hierarchical, cooperative and autonomous – that require leaders to learn the importance of taking time to be self-aware. In the first mode the facilitator takes full responsibility for all major decisions of the learning process; in the second he or she collaborates with the group in devising the learning process; in the third mode of self-directed practice there arises the subtle art of creating conditions within which people can exercise full self-determination in their learning. To cope with the disappointment generated when I don't offer the operating mode that a group may long for, I have been thankful for the work of academic pioneers in this field.

Bill Torbert, Professor of Management at the Carroll School of Management, Boston College, Massachusetts, offers an integrated approach that bridges academic thought and detailed local practice, in which both feed one another on an equal footing. In commending Torbert's *Action Inquiry: The Secret of Timely and Transforming Leadership*, Sandra Waddock (Professor and Galligan Chair of Strategy of Boston College) writes:

> For years now I have watched intense personal and sometimes organizational transformations take place as participants in Boston College's Leadership for Change Program experiment with the ideas that Bill Torbert presents in his book . . . action inquiry can be a path to self and other-awareness, insight and positive changes of the sort that can shape a world in the future that we will all want to live in.

Regardless of anyone's formal position in a group or organization, AI offers a lifelong process for transformational learning for individuals, teams and organizations. Using accessible language and keeping in touch with my own feelings before, during and after meeting with local groups were key ways of guarding against creating just another form of dependency.

PAR methodology subversively aims to make research or the product of knowledge more democratic (see <www.thrive-teesside.org.uk> and <www.church-poverty.org.uk>). It works through sharing questions and the impact and benefits of research. I have found that five factors that characterize PAR provide a constant checklist in my work as companion to local churches:

1 **Practical**
   Who is free to attend?
   What transport is needed?
   Where shall we meet?

Is the space suitable?
What childcare may be needed?
What resources will be needed?
Who will provide them?
2 **Relational**
What confidence do people have in the group?
How will different people feel able to contribute?
What are our agreed practices?
3 **Ethical**
What values are we espousing?
What habits will make sure these values are promoted?
What theories support our work?
4 **Contextual** or **Institutional**
Who is involved?
What constraints or resources are there?
Who has an investment in the work?
To whom are we accountable?
Who is financing this?
5 **Vehicle for change**
Will anything happen?
What partnerships will help?
Who are 'leaders' here?
Who are 'change agents'?
What conversations are most likely to be helpful?

Learning through metaphor

Mary Brydon-Miller (Director of the University of Cincinnati's Action Research Centre) seeks to promote social justice and strengthen communities locally and globally by advancing research, education and action through participatory and reflective practices. At the inaugural meeting of Durham University's Hub for Action Research for Social Justice in April 2015, she illustrated from metaphors the culture she evokes:

• **Jazz** – where music explodes but not randomly; it is the product of hard work, practice and improvisation through time and space.

- **Longitude** – in the mid-eighteenth century, John Harrison, a mere joiner and self-educated clockmaker, solved the longitude problem and so saved many lives. Despite eventually receiving the prize money for his revolutionary timekeepers, he suffered to his death the disrespect of the scientific and academic establishment.
- **The convergence of rivers** – there is creativity and support for human development on all sides when systems mingle. Multiple exposure to different disciplines and methodologies creates a rich dialogue for social change and the generation of knowledge.
- *Indiana Jones and the Last Crusade* – in the challenge to find the Holy Grail, the fictitious unconventional archaeologist steps out on to a bridge that only becomes visible when he trusts it to be there. The bridge rising up under him reminds researchers of the times when they thought no one would turn up or when their trust in one another was at a low ebb.

To be effective, PAR depends on hubs of trust and intimacy where people work together and take risks. I have been fortunate that in this research project many have been willing to become temporary participants in a learning community, where numerous stories came together in one place. I am also encouraged that at its most recent conference on ecclesiology, the Society for the Study of Theology fully embraced the equal standing of experience with Scripture, reason and tradition (<www.theologysociety.org.uk>).

Autoethnography

The discipline of autoethnography has a slightly intimidating name. Essentially it is a route away from the researcher seeming to be a detached observer and recorder of the lives and beliefs of others. It stimulates self-reflection in the researcher – for example: 'How am I experiencing this workshop or conversation?' 'How is my presence making a particular difference?' It is a reminder that no one owns the last word on an interaction on whatever scale. For me its value is in linking with a collaborative theology and practice that recognizes the energy or power of a group or process as a shared responsibility and journey.

Autoethnography has been profoundly valuable for me in this research project. It supports the deliberate and often cautious movement from a traditional objective or foundational way of describing reality to more fluid and flexible language that resonates with contemporary experience. In other words, it subverts the expectation of the expert who can put things right and the power imbalance that inhabits top-down church hierarchical expectations. It has been a support to many participants in finding a new voice that openly challenges the culture and practice of diocesan and local church life and discovering how to introduce innovation. In a very limited way I would claim that my way of being companion with local churches over the past two years, and the writing up of this research by several voices, often revised, reflects the aspirations of autoethnography.

Although the main narrative is owned and expressed by myself, many voices, stories and encounters are included or implied, and the text has been constantly revised in response to new insights. As will become clear in Part 3 of the book, my hope is that this is just the beginning of an extended conversation. Alec Grant (Faculty of Health and Social Science, University of Brighton) and colleagues give expression to this movement:

> The creativity with which autoethnographic pieces are often written opens up a reflexive world in which the researcher/researched join with the reader to create a story. This iterative process of reflection and reflexivity within the autoethnographical process does not lend itself to linear chronological progression, specificity and concreteness; instead, the text might wander, twist and turn, changing direction unexpectedly. It might jump from one thought/feeling/memory or experience up or down or backwards, forwards, sideways to another . . . the story might change, develop and grow throughout the reader's experience of the writing, and almost certainly changes and grows as the author authors and re-authors their writing.
>
> (Grant et al., in Short et al. 2013, p. 2)

This certainly gives voice to my own limited experience of attempting to put in writing something that may be stimulating and resourcing to others but cannot be easily conveyed and actually belongs to scores if not several hundreds of people. There is no escaping that to some high degree as a 'researcher' I am in a privileged position of respect and detachment. Being a 'stranger' is also part of what makes this possible as I can disrupt the vicious circles, say the unsayable and take off the broken record. But what is vital is that, in social science terminology, there has been a 'narrative turn' that is suspicious of some grand explanation of the situation and how to resolve it, a grand plan in which the researcher supposedly remains objective and neutral.

In churches where I have been companion I have seen individuals go through a roller coaster of anxieties about their health, relationships and role; I have seen a community rocked to its core through the dishonesty of a trusted officer – and, not without tears and resentment, rise up again with even more resilience. In other words, to be advocating attentiveness to God's blessing in churches as they are now, and in the relationships that are given, must be firmly grafted onto the present experienced reality, not merely onto organizational or theological 'solutions'.

In the writing up of this research and the advocacy of its findings I have found support in the autoethnographical principles of writing espoused by Judi Marshall (Lancaster University School of Management). I am reminded that I have tidied up the cacophony of voices that inhabit this text and shape the churches I have accompanied. I am also reminded of the limitations of writing, in that 'human meaning is always refracted through the dark looking glass of language, signs and the process of signification' (Grant et al., in Short et al. 2013, p. 7). This story is simply one, among the many, that could have been written, and it therefore remains open for others to make of it what may serve their purposes.

Although this seems a risky and vulnerable approach, my sense is that it fits with the fragile and contingent situation in which most Western churches are now – however much this may be denied out of an anxiety to succeed. Alec Grant's summary of a movement towards a more holistic way of knowing recalls ways of discernment that surely belong so naturally to a community that worships God who comes near as friend, who knows our life is far from easy, that we face significant forces of evil, who inspires us to see more and more of what is going on in our lives and in the world and whose power is shown in crucifixion.

Arguably, academic-, discipline- and profession-based practice based on personal knowledge and experience is more credible, ethical, imbued with integrity, empathic and potentially effective. This marks the difference between implicational and propositional knowledge: between knowing, feeling, connecting and doing, from the heart, based on personal experience, rather than solely on the basis of rationally acquired information.
(Grant et al., in Short et al. 2013, p. 11)

My belief is that the small steps taken in the conversations I have initiated need to be pursued more rigorously and more widely as a credible and valuable way of nurturing whatever futures may be possible for re-imagined patterns of being Church.

3 Storytelling to stimulate transformational conversation

> I am suggesting that what is reported is but one account of an event and consequently representations are unable to be 'the truth'. The 'selves' animated by stories, animate further stories: revising old stories and creating new ones – though whether any story is ever truly new is contestable.
>
> (Arthur Frank, quoted in Short et al. 2013, p. 97)

Working with the cracks

In her poem 'Walking on the Ceiling', Jean Sprackland illustrates the promise of something concealed by imagining a crack in the pavement that fractionally opens wider day by day (Short, in Short et al. 2013, p. 169). It is a gracious loving miracle by God that, despite all our mistakes and lack of faith, and constantly in unexpected forms, episodes of Church continue to emerge, many as brilliant beacons of hope for the world. Beyond ecclesial survival, God invites us to participate in being Church as signs and foretastes of God's constancy, desire and love for all and for the healing of the world.

In my experience as companion, walking alongside church communities and ordained ministers, I do not cease to be surprised at how unforeseen newness arises. We find it hard sometimes even to admit there is a problem. To be vulnerably open to God's future requires that we live in a real sense of being blessed beyond our deserts or expectations. For leaders and preachers this involves persistently reminding ourselves and others of the Spirit's power that runs between us in the furrows of organizational and personal existence.

One of the tasks of leadership is to invite people into conversations that matter, believing in God's surprising ways of nudging people and communities to move from a preoccupation with deficit to a trust that something new – blessing – can burst out. That's not to say there aren't struggles between those who see a need to remake patterns of

Church and those who are more loyal to past practices and ancestors. And we know from, say, the work of the practical theologian Jean Vanier (2009, p. 103) or the Appreciative Inquiry (AI) pioneer Diana Whitney (Whitney and Trosten-Bloom 2003, p. 29), that healing and development in institutions is all one with the healing and development of people and communities.

Here are two examples of churches of different denominations and national settings beginning to discover how, through conversation, they can move beyond dependency on clergy and beyond the fear of collapse, to an emerging future.

Unhooking from the past

The first is the story of a group of Lutheran churches in the Western Nassau Conference, New York (Evangelical Lutheran Church in America – ELCA), with whom I have been an occasional companion for over a decade. Richard Hill, an experienced church leader and consultant, tells how he has always seen his primary role as that of 'building up the church' and teaching congregations to live as a community of the baptized. Richard recognizes, however, that like many other churches worldwide, the profile of its members is increasingly elderly, the numbers of worshippers are decreasing and there is an urgency to rediscover how to share the gospel of Christ in contemporary society.

Practitioners of Participatory Action Research make it a priority to be as self-aware as possible and to be cautious of the delusion that we can ever be detached observers. So, fascinating as our account may be of the dynamics in a given congregation, the assessment by Richard and myself is inevitably limited. It is, quite literally, a view from a single point: that of two clerics with many years of experience and whose theologies of Church overlap in many areas (Whitney and Trosten-Bloom 2003, pp. 183ff.).

Having established the limitations of an 'expert' consultant's observation, Richard notices some characteristics of Lutheran churches in Western Nassau:

- uneasy relationships between pastors and people;
- churches no longer able to fund their own pastor;

- churches with money but no sense of direction;
- serious illness among clergy;
- churches sharing a pastor without a commitment of the ministry of all;
- pioneer clergy disconnected from others.

His sense that local churches were living with a high degree of uncertainty and lack of missional energy was largely corroborated in a workshop at which 60 church members voiced their own reading of the situation through AI conversation, to which I was companion in May 2015.

Richard's reading of the situation includes the following points:

- Our congregations participate in a system that used to work, more or less.
- For most churches this requires the services of seminary-trained ordained leaders who perform specific roles as full-time pastors in individual congregational settings on behalf of the laity.
- These pastors are assisted in their pastoral work, more or less, by individual lay members who volunteer to serve on a part-time basis, often without any significant preparation, ongoing support, continuing ministerial education, public affirmation or pastoral supervision.
- Given the difficulties of managing people's daily schedules and the lack of experience of our clergy in belonging to ministry teams, these volunteer ministers are often not invited to take part in exercising their ministries as members of ministry teams.
- The situation is well summed up in the saying: 'The system is perfectly designed to achieve the results it is getting.'
- The turning point is when the Church as a whole agrees to ask the question: 'What is the role of a pastor in a contemporary Lutheran congregation?'
- In most churches there is an expectation that the ordained minister will usually preach and preside, teach (at least the youth), offer pastoral care and support to members (and others living locally) in times of illness and personal crisis, marry, bury and attend meetings.
- Although such roles have been performed by clergy for many generations, some clergy add other items to their lists of priorities and find satisfaction in doing them. This will depend on past role models, teaching or personal competence, but many of these things

often turn out to be simply a personal choice, neither specifically for building up the body of Christ locally nor the result of congregational consultation.

- Wider experience and research indicate that for churches to grow into their identity as mission and ministering bodies of disciples requires purposeful choices and quantities of dedicated time. Such processes are frustrated when clergy draw up their own job descriptions as outlined above.
- The pressure is even more acute in synods or dioceses where each church is expected to be financially self-sustaining.

One Saturday at the end of 2014, after a year of conversations between pastors and leaders of the ten congregations of the Western Nassau Conference, 65 people came together at Gloria Dei Lutheran Church in New Hyde Park for their first 'Vision Day'. The event was initiated by a special conference steering committee and planned by a leadership team, with Richard as companion. It was the culmination of several months of discussions among the pastors and lay leaders of the Western Nassau Conference, who are taking part in a pilot project initiated by the Gathered Committee of the Metro New York Synod's Strategic Planning process.

Leaders identified needs and opportunities for congregations that are working together to plan for the future. This event marked the first formal effort to bring leaders together for conversations around the topic 'Creating our shared future together'. Following reflection and prayer and a presentation, participants held conversations to consider the future in three 'clusters'.

Although the challenges faced by each cluster group were strikingly different, they found sufficient mutual respect to recognize that together they have opportunities for sharing in ministry together. As one commented, 'Now we can start exploring those opportunities in a significant way.'

At the time of writing there have been many setbacks through illness, resignations and even death. Richard sees the events of recent months as the beginning of long process, in which the local churches will share: 'There will be no rescue mission from outside. They will have to work out the future together.' As the synod consultant, he will continue to assist leaders in expanding the congregations by form-ing small teams in three clusters that will bring leaders together in future months for further conversations. So here is no 'success' story that proves the value of AI or transformational conversation – as a programme. Rather it seems like a realization that only a death to trusting in old patterns of dependency, only the embracing of a God vulnerable and defenceless can bring about a fresh and renewed performance of the communities we call 'church'. The subversive call of Brueggemann, referring to the scriptural drama of three days, needs to ring in our conventional ears as:

> a script for 'guerrilla theatre', an endlessly available re-enactment, retelling, rehearing, redescribing, reperformance that issues a surprise reading against every settled human world [inviting us to move]:
>
> - out of {*denial*} that imagines an endlessly triumphant God;
> - out of {*despair*} that imagines an endlessly defeated God;
> - out of {*complacency*} that imagines a returned God as a house pet.
>
> (Brueggemann 2002, pp. 119–20)

Forward together in hope

The second story is of two Roman Catholic parishes in the North-East of England, with a generally negative or even disengaged response to the new reality of being made, by the Diocese of Hexham, to share one parish priest. It has been painful for long-established congregations no longer to have their own priest or the residential ministry of religious sisters. The church where the priest does not live has naturally experienced greater bereavement. Apart from direct church responsibilities, Fr David also makes a significant contribution to two primary and one secondary Catholic schools. Recent health concerns have caused him to reduce the overall energy he puts into his working week.

For 18 months, while I have been in conversation with members of both congregations and their priest, the critical question has been: 'How do we attract and support younger people to be part of our churches?' The consistent expectation has been that it's the priest's role to achieve this.

Repeatedly, Fr David had preached about being Church as the baptized and confirmed body of Christ, and asked the congregations to recommend names of those who might become leaders. During months of feeling unwell and undergoing hospital tests, his experience was that very few responded to his pleas or those of the workshops we had run together. We discussed how, if the congregations wouldn't hear about the churches' dilemmas from their own priest, they would hardly take time to work with an Anglican visitor.

Then suddenly Fr David arrived at one of our occasional meetings in the railway-station café, full of joy that one of the parish pastoral councils had decided to move beyond lament into new practices of ministry. He was overwhelmed when the parish council at the church where he was not resident described how, without telling him, they had held a market place of ministries. Stalls had been set up and refreshments offered. Each stall was staffed by people who wanted to recruit others to different aspects of mission and ministry. Ten new members of the congregation – some of them quite young – had been recruited. 'So they did hear me!' exclaimed Fr David. He wrote in an email: 'I'm delighted by this new beginning. It's Easter! It's the beginning of the end of assuming that only the clergy can deal with spiritual matters.'

He began to reflect that maybe his recent months of illness had been the trigger for people to listen to him and maybe to God, rather than to theological 'truths' about baptismal ministry. Here we noted that this account of events, while powerful, was limited to guesswork and to finding a way for two clerics to make sense of a painful situation. 'In that case it doesn't look like a good strategy,' said Fr David at our next meeting, 'but at least they've decided to stop living in the tomb created for laity centuries ago.' In the same parish church he described how he had set examples – by showing what is possible with a more prominent Christmas crib, and in the other church he served by displaying international flags around the church for Pentecost. 'Is this for the World Cup, Father?' asked one parishioner. 'Well, maybe it is!' The point is that discipleship is about life in the world. 'How can laity come to Mass and then not challenge the culture of loan sharks? How can they be season-ticket holders and not insist that corruption can't promote good soccer?' But we shared the joy of a waking up to God's blessing with a future full of promise.

Fr David continues the story at Easter 2015, by which time it had been put in the narrative told by the wider context of his diocese:

Both parishes are beginning a journey of discovery and discernment along with the rest of the Diocese of Hexham, facing wholesale changes in the way of being Church in different localities. The challenge facing all clergy and laity is allowing God to be God to us, to transform us through the very issues we face, to become disciples and cease to be passive consumers of religious services.

As we celebrate Holy Week and Easter together we need to go through our Gethsemane, walk through our passion and do a lot of dying to self, burying everything which no longer helps in the mission field, and be emptied enough to receive the resurrection life God wants us to be blessed with. Having been formed by an education and culture where we feel the need to have the map and plan, and therefore be in control, this calls for faith in God who alone has the map and plan, and only gives enough light for the day or just a few steps ahead.

Like Moses and the Hebrews in the wilderness, or the Apostles after Pentecost, Fr David thinks we're especially called to become Christian mystics to rise up for the challenges ahead, as Karl Rahner foresaw in the last century. The remnant that remains faithful will be a blessing from God to transform the world, potent leaven furthering God's kingdom.

I hope that these particular stories, limited as they are, have been enough to make you impatient to begin conversations of your own and at your own pace.

To be challenged by God and others is to know their love – they have not given up on us! God may sometimes be justly angry with us, as part of our endless relationship and transformation. We could come to welcome moments when we feel confronted or surprised, open to the changes God may be asking of us. And we must look after one another. Sharing our deepest feelings about God and God's work among us can bring a sense of freedom and happiness but also a realistic fear of being shamed or let down. So I ask you: 'Please don't end the conversations when you finish this book.' My hope is that it will be just the beginning of a more enlivened pathway for you and your church.

PART 2

FIVE CONVERSATIONS FOR CHANGING CHURCHES ON THE THEME OF BLESSING

4 Opening the door

> You call us all to live, and see good days,
> Centre in Christ and enter his peace,
> To seek his Way amongst our many ways,
> Find Blessedness in Blessing, peace in praise,
> To clear and keep for Love, a sacred space
> That we might be beginners in God's grace.
> ('A Sonnet for St Benedict', in Guite 2013)

The spirit of conversation

Here are five outline conversations on blessing, designed to accompany you as you seek to renew your practice of Church as blessed and blessing. Through a growing presence to God, one another, society and creation, expect to be led to:

- a spirit of mutual affirmation arising from gratitude;
- lament at the world's pain;
- renewed understanding of your faith and appreciation of one another;
- new possibilities, arising from conversation;
- fresh energy for seeing an old 'problem' in a new light.

These won't come in a neat linear way but unpredictably; through your willingness to be as *present* as possible. Assessing where you and your church are now, you will be invited to travel together towards God's future calling for you all.

Each conversation requires a minimum of one and a half to two hours. You may decide to allow one conversation to last for several meetings or to space out the conversations over weeks or months.

Whatever you are facing, together and alone consider the following:

- How can you increasingly experience yourselves as a community blessed by God?

- How can you bless God more fully in the life of your church?
- How can you go beyond previous limitations and doubts?
- How can your church become more of a blessing to others, locally or globally?

The experience of these conversations will I hope encourage you to continue to integrate this approach by creating more conversations to address your needs as you discover renewed ways of being Church.

The role of the companion

In my experience, churches that have had the benefit of external consultancy have discovered fresh confidence to make the changes they realize need to happen. In group processes designed to envisage the future of churches, the role of facilitator is not the same as hosting or leading a group; rather it is *walking with* and inviting the group into a culture that includes respect and mutuality, in which everyone takes responsibility in some way. There are always at least four elements to be noticed and gently aligned:

- The task that the group has been given for the organization.
- The personal development of each participant.
- Awareness of the power dynamics at play.
- Discerning how to respond in the moment to the unexpected.

To become more adept at making such judgements skilfully is to develop an 'ability to judge the fitting action to take within multiple possibilities and uncertainties' (Christine Oliver and Graham Brittain, quoted in Lewis et al. 2008, p. 127). Personal gifts and experience have made some people naturals in this role of walking with a group. Instinctively they know how to be fully engaged at the same time as keeping an eye out for the four key tasks to be creatively woven together. For others this will be more of a learned art.

'Companion' is the best word I can think of to use for this role. Literally, it refers to one who shares bread with us. So he or she is both part of the group and has a particular role. The companion needs to be one who wants the 'bread' that is shared to be made slowly and carefully by everyone present. Attractive words associated with truly nourishing bread might be 'organic', 'fresh' and 'locally sourced'. In other words, the companion is not one who will force the pace, offer old solutions from his or her own experience, ignore the actual people in the room or forget the very specific context in which these conversations are taking place.

It is, for me, an enjoyable though demanding role, and difficult to describe or define on paper. I believe many can grow the necessary skills and attitudes by practice and through reflection, review and encouragement. It seems to work best if companions have a certain detachment through perhaps being borrowed from a neighbouring church – and perhaps having learned appropriate skills at work. The more detached position of being an outsider, for example, makes it easier, with humour and gentleness, to challenge people and the group about the recycling of stories and attitudes that block movement forward. But given the realities of most churches, groups will be grateful that someone is prepared to give it their best concentration and love.

I've chosen to use the term 'companion' rather than 'facilitator' to emphasize that the benefits of the process of change are of the same character as the change we are intending to bring about. I understand the work of companionship to be the deliberate and gradual relinquishing of control of a group in order to encourage new energy and confidence through conversation and the group's growing capacity to hold a conversational space. This requires that the companion is secure enough in herself or himself to trust the people in the conversation

- to learn the art of good listening to one another, rather than just waiting to talk;
- to focus on others rather than themselves;
- to listen to what they are themselves saying and to monitor how often they speak;

- to listen for new ideas that are emerging in the room;
- to support one another in becoming better listeners.

The Apostle Paul inspired groups of disciples to recognize themselves as fully functioning churches, filled with all the gifts and skills they needed. He instilled into them the values and purpose of Christian community; he trusted them to discover the leadership that would sustain and guide them locally; and he occasionally visited, and often corresponded, stimulating their confidence and courage in responding to God's mission in particular situations. He would be well versed in social media in today's world. Having had the intensive two-year experience of being companion to a range of very different churches, I am increasingly convinced of the value for all churches of having appropriate external support and stimulus as the norm. And I know that this may often seem difficult to achieve.

The role of companion does require certain skills, but it seems mainly to require a particular attitude that, for me, is rooted in the notion of trust; that is, trust in the power and fidelity of God and in God's people, the local church. Paul trusted local churches to desire more of God's purposes for them and to respond to information.

We are reminded in Ecclesiastes (3.1–8) that every season has its own requirements. Now I believe passionately that the present moment requires churches, regionally, to be developing 'companionship' for changing churches. Churches and leaders, regionally, need to discern who can fulfil this role in their churches. How can the generous exchange of resources within churches be expanded to include this vital ministry of companionship in change? There is a need for dioceses to recruit, train and make available those who can be effective companions.

My concern is whether the role can be sufficiently described in a book. I am aware of having had the privilege over decades of learning the art of companionship by watching and working with others. I would not be alone in naming with gratitude David Durston, Malcolm Grundy and other group-process pioneers within the Edward King Institute for Ministerial

Development (EKI). The movement triggered by EKI in the 1980s and 1990s, now combined with current person-centred approaches to organizational culture, points out deficiencies in the churches' responses to addressing the urgent management of change. In my recent research I have recognized that beyond skill is the question of trust – how can one intentionally be a companion for churches so as to increase their confidence, reduce their dependency and trust their own emerging voice? Paraphrasing John the Baptizer's position with regard to his relationship with Jesus, 'He must increase while I decrease'.

> A companion is one with whom one shares bread. God calls his people to be his companions, the ones with whom he shares bread – his friends.   (Samuel Wells 2006, p. 1)

In churches in the UK and in the USA, where an earlier form of this material has been used, the vital role of companion has been recognized. The road-testing process has also highlighted the difficulty of finding people willing and able to take on this role for another church. The groups were looking for fellow Christian travellers, preferably with the detachment of coming from a neighbouring church – someone who had at least some of the gifts of humility, the ability to 'read' a situation, being approachable, accepting what is, compassion, and patience as events unfold. Churches regionally could make a positive difference by identifying and making known potential companions for local churches.

Some key responsibilities of the companion

These include:

- to work with the church's leaders to develop a clear framework of aims and objectives consistent with the material in this book;
- to negotiate with a group from the start ground rules and expectations, including confidentiality;
- to be prepared to hold boundaries for the group, ensuring its safety for all and its openness to creativity and the unexpected;

- to assist exchanges within the group with sensitivity, while challenging them when appropriate;
- to watch out for and listen to the participants and the dynamic of the group – when someone talks over others or takes up a disproportionate amount of the time, the companion may need to suggest sensitively that others also need to be heard;
- to expect the unexpected and be alert to going with the flow as well as defending the group from being dominated by an individual or pair;
- to balance the planned process, the needs of the group and the contribution of participants while choosing when to follow a lead off the map for a while;
- to encourage everyone to take responsibility for the liveliness and health of the group, for example by reading through the material for each meeting in advance and being willing to volunteer to read or contribute towards refreshments, as they are able;
- initially to lead group prayers and arrange for material to be photocopied, but then to move deliberately into a background position, drawing out others' confidence;
- to gradually lead the group to trust in silence as well as in their own voice – if someone makes it clear that at first they'd just prefer to listen, that must be respected;
- to be a listening ear to anyone who needs to continue reflecting on something that has come up in the conversation – or to make sure that an appropriate contact is made with a church leader or friend.

All this may seem too much. Each companion, with his or her own particular skills and aptitude, will do what is possible! Indeed as time goes on and confidence builds in a group, the need for interventions will decrease. Filling this role with sensitivity brings immense rewards. Companions can experience a deep sense of accomplishment when the group generates laughter, tears, friendship and a sense of new confidence. My hope is that in developing this role the companions will become a resource for the future as well as deepening the capacity of their local church to listen and connect their lives to the active presence of God in the world. 'May the God of hope fill you with all joy and peace in believing, so that you may abound in hope by the power of the Holy Spirit' (Rom. 15.13).

Advance planning

This will include:

- Who will take part? Who is recruiting? Clarify the make-up of the group (e.g. gender, age, abilities, commitment).
- What will your church and the participants gain from taking part?
- If the conversations are to be fully productive, experience suggests that words alone will be insufficient. Some physical movement or activity needs to be introduced. The varied resources in Macy and Brown's *Coming Back to Life* (2013) may offer a lead into this.
- Do you or participants have special interests (e.g. music or art) that could develop the material provided and make it more accessible?
- Decide beforehand how you will use the material. How much of it? Will you make it available to everyone or not?
- Where will the group meet and who will be the host? Consider how the group's interactive power may be affected by this territorial decision. Would a neutral space be an advantage?
- Consider whether the chosen date and time will make it possible for people to attend (depending on the time of day and location) or if it conflicts with some other commitment of the local church.
- What 'contract' do you have with church leaders and participants to make genuine time and energy for this process and to monitor its progress?
- What style will you bring to the sessions? How will you meet your needs as companion for this learning? Companions need periodic support from someone with the capacity to

understand the dynamic of the group or able to help consider alternative ways to present some part of the material.

(Adapted from Rifkin 2010, pp. 21–2)

The role of the host

Church council members or leaders will need to invite someone to host each conversation group – whether in church premises, a home or somewhere else. The host:

- needs to create a suitable space, in consultation with the companion;
- arranges that 15 minutes before the meeting is due to begin there are sufficient chairs arranged so that everyone can see one another's faces and the temperature is comfortable;
- makes sure everyone is greeted by name and that people can be reminded of one another's names in the way that seems best;
- watches out sensitively for anyone who leaves the group without warning or who joins after the group has initially formed;
- can invite others to share in the provision of whatever refreshments are decided upon (throughout the conversation outlines there are reminders of these tasks);
- negotiates with the companion whether there will there be music playing, perhaps a lighted candle;
- checks if anyone would be glad of a lift to and from the group.

To follow the God of Jesus Christ means to worship him, to be his friends, and to eat with him: in short to be his companions: that is the nature and destiny of humankind.

(Samuel Wells 2006, p. 1)

Practicalities to consider in advance

The host and the companion:

- will have met previously and familiarized themselves with the positive approaches to holistic change explored in Part 1;

- will meet at some point after the meeting – or speak on the phone or by email – to review how it went and to make plans for next time;
- will decide whether to create a simple summary sheet for participants, making selective use of the material provided (will it include the text of Scripture passages referred to in each conversation?).

The host:

- will negotiate with church leaders on how people are to be drawn into the group;
- will carefully prepare the space for the meeting and be ready in good time to welcome people by name as they arrive;
- will decide if there will be refreshments before starting, during the meeting or afterwards, and how that will enhance the whole experience.

Opening a conversation

At the advertised time, the host welcomes everyone, including the companion.

The companion helps the group agree about when the meeting will close, explaining that it will be possible for any who wish to stay on a while longer.

Who are we? It cannot be assumed that everyone will know the names of others. The companion leads the group in getting to know each other. This can be done by inviting each person to say their name. They might add some brief words of self-introduction and say what they're hoping for or anxious about – *this is an exercise in listening not a discussion! Essentially it sets a tone for how the group will interact.*

Group practice

The companion:

- briefly explains to the group the purpose and style of the conversations;

- invites the group to recognize that churches always have critical questions and that these conversations may be a good place to consider such questions;
- helps the group to make a pact of confidentiality: we may take away anything we learn about God, ourselves, faith and church – but nothing personal about others in the group;
- encourages each member of the group to take responsibility for how things go by reading through the material for each meeting in advance and being willing to volunteer to read or contribute toward refreshments as she or he is able;
- makes available large-font copies of the Scripture reading and any other material chosen.

Welcome to a learning journey

Let me, for a moment, open the door into a conversation. Clustered around a space sit seven or eight people at different stages on the Christian journey. They might be in someone's home, a pub, a shop, a church, a prison or a school. At the centre of the circle, on a coloured cloth, lies an informal arrangement of a lighted candle, a cross, a picture and an open book of the Gospels. As music fades away, someone offers a prayer, inviting the Holy Spirit's active presence. The group sing or listen perhaps to one of Bernadette Farrell's interpretations of a psalm. They listen carefully to a Scripture passage and begin a conversation with God and with one another on living as God's beloved ones, in order to be a blessing to others.

- Here is a place to talk *with*, rather than be talked *at*.
- Here is a time to be present to one another in the light of God's abundant ways with the world.
- Here is an opportunity to slow down and ask again how to respond to God's call.
- Here it's normal to be vulnerable, doubting, struggling and discovering. Mary, now in her eighties, laments cheerfully, 'I thought that when I got to my age, all would become clear. But it hasn't.'

- Here, untidily, are acceptance, laughter, tears, excitement and hope.

The Franciscan friar Richard Rohr concisely sums up the new opportunities for communal learning in a time when we are recognizing the limitations of passive, individualistic and merely head-centred education:

> The form of education which most changes people in lasting ways has to touch them at a broader level than the thinking, reading mind can do. Somehow we need to engage in hands-on experience, emotional risk-taking, moving outside our comfort zones, with different people than our usual flattering friends. We need some expanded level of spiritual seeing or nothing really changes at a cellular or emotional level. Within minutes of entertaining a new idea, we quickly return to our old friends, our assured roles, our familiar neural grooves, our ego patterns of response, and we are back in business as usual.
>
> (Adapted from Rohr 2012, pp. 43–4)

A pilgrim prayer

Go

  Although your spirit may not know where
  your feet will carry your heart,

Go

  Another is coming to meet you,
  and is searching for you
  so that you can find him in the sanctuary
  at the end of the pilgrimage,
  in the sanctuary deep inside your heart.

  ('He Is Your Peace, He Is Your Peace',
  carried by a South African pilgrim and
  presented at Refugio Gaucelmo, in
  Müller and de Aránguiz 2010, p. xxix)

5 Conversation 1: What is blessing?

The archetypal scriptural notion of blessing is found in the call of Abraham – 'in you all the families of the earth shall be blessed' (Genesis 12.3). The fulfillment of blessing comes in finding one has been a blessing to others.

(Samuel Wells 2006, p. 221)

Loving Father, we thank you for our lives, our faith and this opportunity to talk together. May your Spirit surround and encourage us as we meet and help us to listen to you and to one another. We pray in Jesus' name. **Amen**.

Learning to abide in God's love

As the Father has loved me,
so I have loved you; abide in my love.
If you keep my commandments,
you will abide in my love,
just as I have kept my Father's
commandments and abide in his love.

I have said these things to you
so that my joy may be in you,
and that your joy may be complete . . .
I do not call you servants any longer,
because the servant does not know
what the master is doing;
but I have called you friends,
because I have made known to you
everything that I have heard from my Father.

(John 15.9–11, 15)

Someone in the group reads this passage slowly.

In a time of quiet, the companion invites everyone to pick a word that especially stands out.

After three minutes all are invited to tell the others – without interruption – which words they chose, and why. The passage is read a second time, and the companion invites a short exchange of responses and questions.

Food for the journey: blessing in everyday speech

In two groups, remember together phrases we often hear used about blessing. See how many you can add to this list.

- Bless you! (to save our soul escaping when we sneeze!)
- Bless! (on seeing someone coping despite problems).
- It was a mixed blessing.
- She was blessed with a strong singing voice.
- We were blessed with this terrible manager at work.
- Count your blessings!
- I'm blessed if I know!

Consider together for a minute or two:

- When have you felt blessed?
- When have others told you that you have been a blessing to them?

Now take a few moments to exchange your stories of blessing, paying careful and respectful attention to each person. When everyone has shared their experience, what positive questions might help to deepen their learning?

Take a break – time for refreshments?

Blessing in Scripture

Below is a brief reminder of how some of our ancestors in faith have lived in blessing.

For ten minutes, in twos or threes, choose one of the following passages and themes. Then share your findings.

- **Beloved** – knowing that we are God's beloved: believed in, desired and affirmed by God (Luke 1.41–45, 46–47; 10.21–24; 11.28; 24.52–53).

- **Liberated** – the intimate movement between God and all creation (Eph. 1.3–14); God exercising power and respecting human freedom.
- **God recreating the world** – God's present activity in the world, inviting human participation (Gen. 1.26–30; 2.18–19; Luke 24.47–53; Acts 3.25–26).
- **God for us** – God bringing newness through affirming and building up rather than threatening and defending against others (Luke 6.27–42; 23.24; Rom. 11.32; 12.14).
- **Transformation** – a breaking through to hope, reconciliation, service and joy. It is to be followers of Jesus in referring the whole of our living and dying to God the Father, in the most intimate way imaginable. Jesus refers to the Father as loving, generous, and boundlessly forgiving (Matt. 4.23–25; 10.40; 11.27; 18.15; John 15.15; Heb. 2.9, 14–18; 7.25, 27; 12.22–28).
- **Commissioning** – after the resurrection, Jesus entrusts the disciples with his own work, based on the pattern of his ministry. Fear and joy, praise and worship create an intensity that is a force for the world's flourishing (Matt. 28.8–9, 17; Luke 24.41, 52).
- **Community of God's beloved** – a community of unique disciples are called to be one in Christ, each delighting in the other to bring hope to the world (Matt. 6.12; John 13.20; 15.13; 17.17–19, 20–23; 21.15–17; Acts 2.43–47; Rom. 5.2–5; 1 Cor. 14.1; Eph. 1.3–14; Gal. 3.28; Col. 1.24; Heb. 13.15–16).
- **Eucharistic living** – to bless God is to enjoy and thank God for all our benefits and healing, as ways of being drawn towards God (Luke 17.11–19). The Rabbis of Jesus' day used to teach that to benefit from food or shelter without blessing God was to rob God. Small eucharistic communities grow into and reveal a world transfigured in Christ.

(Note to the companion: you may choose to use this material over the course of more than one meeting and adapt the suggested timings as needed.)

The whole of Jesus' ministry, to the cross and beyond, was a demonstration of God's overwhelming blessing, against the odds. Reflect on these passages:

> I have said all these things to you while I am still with you. But the Advocate, the Holy Spirit, whom the Father will send in my name, will teach you everything, and remind you of all that I have said to you. (John 14.25–26)

> In the last days it will be, God declares,
> that I will pour out my Spirit upon all flesh,
> and your sons and your daughters will prophesy,
> and your young men shall see visions,
> and your old men shall dream dreams.
> (Acts 2.17)

In twos and threes, take one or two of the following questions and then share with the others:

- What would it mean for us to be the corporate body of the risen Christ – resonating with the words 'The Lord is here!' in us?
- How can we amaze ourselves by becoming a blessing to all those among whom we live?
- How does it help to recall that, thankfully, it is God who creates us as Church, occasionally with some help from us?
- What is your response to the idea that blessing – which includes praise, joy, thanksgiving, happiness, the final beatitude of creation – and our sense of being loved by God is the vital springboard for any plans we may have for making a better job of being Church?
- How far do you agree with the idea that God gives us more than enough to be God's friends and witnesses?
- If you think you don't believe you have enough 'ministry', would it help to consider whether you're looking in the right place?

In the group:

- Tell of one thing we are especially proud of about our church life.

- In turn, ask each person how our church could become even more of a blessing.
- What else would be needed?
- Where would we find it?

A critical question

This is not intended to invite criticism of someone, some group or even 'the church'. It is asking 'What is an issue for our church and/or locality that urgently needs our creative attention?'

Today we make a start noting the critical question(s) our church identifies.

Does the group agree on a question or does it see a more urgent one?

The companion invites everyone to say something about this and be ready to talk more about it next time.

Review

Each person has a short time to say what has been the most important moment for him or her in this conversation.

What do you hope for in the conversations that follow?

Closing prayer

The companion leads a final prayer, the Lord's Prayer, and ends:

The grace and mercy of our Lord Jesus Christ be with you.
The Lord bless you

The meeting is now closed, so that people are free to go or stay and talk a while longer.

For next time, please read Matthew 5.3–10, The Beatitudes. Reflect on how, when we alter how we look at familiar things, the things themselves start to look different (Dyer, in Laloux 2014, p. 41).

6   Conversation 2: Living in praise

Praise of God is not necessary, it is an overflow, a generous extravagance of response which is easily seen as useless and deluded.

(Ford and Hardy 2005, p. 15)

Opening the conversation

Who are we?
   The host welcomes everyone.

Group practice

The companion:

- helps the group to welcome anyone new and notice if anyone has not yet arrived;
- invites people to remind one another of their names;
- asks people to say one thing about the previous conversation;
- reminds the group of the brief introduction last time to the idea of a 'critical question', one of the urgent issues every church faces in one way or another. The suggestion is that in conversations of this kind, rooted in knowing we are blessed, a deeper response might begin to emerge.

What were the suggestions last time about our critical question?

- how to reach new people;
- how to be a greater blessing to the local neighbourhood;
- respecting different views within your church;
- being wary of change . . . or whatever your issue might be.

Which critical question(s) seem most important to the group?

Experiencing God's outpouring love

In those days Jesus came from Nazareth of Galilee and was baptized by John in the Jordan. And just as he was coming up out of the water, he saw the heavens torn apart and the Spirit descending like a dove on him. And a voice came from heaven, 'You are my Son, the Beloved; with you I am well pleased.'

(Mark 1.9–11)

Jesus experiences an outpouring of God's love. It launches his ministry. Jesus invites us to know ourselves also as daughters and sons of the Father, equally blessed.

Prayer

We pray together.

> Creating and healing God,
> thank you for drawing us together again
> to listen to you and to one another
> and to the cries of the world.
> Fill us with your blessing;
> overcome our deaf ears
> with your transforming words and presence.
> Reach into our tiredness and anxiety;
> kindle a flame of hope in us again.
> Draw us nearer to you and so to all your creatures.
> We are ready to listen and speak. **Amen**.

Food for the journey: receiving and giving praise

• What does it mean to 'live in praise'?
• Is praising God a waste of time when we could be usefully doing something?

Think in twos – for a few minutes – about when you have been praised or have praised others.

• What effect did these experiences have on you?
• What difference does it make when you praise others?

For about ten minutes the whole group shares experiences and responses and considers:

- If every thing, person and movement has its origin in God's blessing, blessing is the ultimate source.
- To take God as at the heart of all things is to live in blessing.

In twos, take one of the following Scripture references. Ask yourselves: 'What does it add to our conversation on blessing':

- to know that we too are accepted as God's beloved (Matt. 3.17; Mark 1.11; Luke 3.22; 2 Pet. 1.17)?
- to be drawn into the same mutual relationship that Jesus has with his Father (John 17.1–10)?
- to refer all things to the Father (see especially Mark 14.36, but implied in all Jesus' teaching; Rom. 8.15; Gal. 4.6)?
- to give glory to God in the middle of all of life's experiences (Hab. 3.19; Matt. 6.14; John 15.5)?
- to experience joy and pleasure through worship of God who is the source of all joy?
- to be changed 'from glory to glory' (2 Cor. 3.16–18)?
- to be renewed in energy (Ps. 91 and Isa. 40.31)?

Praising God in worship

In the whole group, choose one or two of the following to continue the conversation:

- **Singing** – significant words that bind Christians together and liberate our whole person and common life;
- **Adoration** – as being still and silent with God; contemplative practice connects us with all others who pray and with all creation;
- **Penitence** – recognizing sin as the blocking of deeper communion with God;
- **Intercession** – assuming a loving God who is actively involved in the details of human living;

- **Sacrament** – praise as expressed in baptism, confirmation, confession, anointing of the sick, ordination, marriage and in a huge variety of ways and understandings; the central mystery of Christian praise is focused in the Eucharist (or Lord's Supper, Holy Communion or the Mass);
- **Spontaneity** – praise overflowing as healing, revival and renewal.

Experiencing God coming close

For about five minutes in twos, and ten minutes in the whole group, recall and tell of a particular time or place when you experienced God with your whole selves.

Break for refreshments.

Revisiting a critical question

A thread through these conversations is to keep returning to our critical question(s). Consider again the suggestions of last time. Can we narrow them down to a single question on which to focus in the weeks ahead? Agree to hold this in mind in the context of blessing and praise and recognizing God at the heart of reality.

As a way of going deeper, consider:

- What is key to our way of being Church?
- Do most local people consider themselves to be Christian?
- What hopes does God have for us as Church in this area?

Knowing our deepest selves

Read Philippians 1.3–20 – in three voices.

I thank my God every time I remember you, constantly praying with joy in every one of my prayers for all of you, because of your sharing in the gospel from the first day until now. I am confident of this, that the one who began a good work among you will bring it to completion by the day of Jesus Christ.

It is right for me to think this way about all of you, because you hold me in your heart, for all of you share in God's grace with me, both in my imprisonment and in the defence and confirmation of the gospel. For God is my witness, how I long for all of you with the compassion of Christ Jesus.

And this is my prayer, that your love may overflow more and more with knowledge and full insight to help you to determine what is best, so that on the day of Christ you may be pure and blameless, having produced the harvest of righteousness that comes through Jesus Christ for the glory and praise of God.

What themes emerge for you?

Prompts for conversation:

- transformation of the community through astonished joy in Christ;
- God's glory, rejoicing and loving;
- praise and joy as central not optional to Christian practice;
- in what ways have you or others grown through suffering?

Review

In twos, for five minutes, consider:

- What insights have come to you in this conversation?
- What are you hoping for?
- What troubled you or seemed unhelpful?
- Who has not been here? Who might contact them with sensitivity?

Closing prayer

Hold in prayer one thing from each person that has been important.

Pray together

> Holy God, help us now –
> to give our lives
> to give our love
> to give our minds

to give ourselves – to you
through Jesus Christ our Lord. **Amen.**

The grace and mercy of our Lord Jesus Christ be with you.
The Lord Bless you, Amen.

Tasks for next time: read the outline of Conversation 3
(next chapter); be ready to read; pray; or prepare to bring
refreshments.

7 Conversation 3: Church as a wisdom community

Healthy ministry flows out of genuine charisms – honestly recognized and generously shared . . . a source of joy, a deep consolation that carries one through all the craziness and conflict, all the disagreements and disappointments . . . the delight that God is simply delighting in our response, 'Yes! That's what I made you for!'

(Hahnenberg 2014, p. 84)

Who are we?

- Welcome anyone new, notice who has not yet arrived. Does everyone know the names of those in the group?
- Consider how an event of recent days has been a blessing.
- Receive any reflections from last time.

Prayer

Lord, we thank you for our lives
and for your presence among us now.
Be close to us as we share our feelings and thoughts
And show us how to share the good news of your resurrection.
Amen.

Where do we live?

Today we're going to start the conversation by considering the spaces where we live. This will mean different things to different people here.

In threes, and then in the group, consider:

- Who lives nearest to the church building? Who lives furthest away?

- Who has lived here longest? Who is the latest arrival?

Again in threes and then in the group, ask:

- What do we appreciate most about living here?
- How would you recommend it to someone else?
- What would improve living here?

Dynamic Bible study: Moses' encounter with God

Several voices read:

> Moses was keeping the flock of his father-in-law Jethro, the priest of Midian; he led his flock beyond the wilderness, and came to Horeb, the mountain of God. There the angel of the LORD appeared to him in a flame of fire out of a bush; he looked, and the bush was blazing, yet it was not consumed. Then Moses said, 'I must turn aside and look at this great sight, and see why the bush is not burned up.' When the LORD saw that he had turned aside to see, God called to him out of the bush, 'Moses, Moses!' And he said, 'Here I am.' Then he said, 'Come no closer! Remove the sandals from your feet, for the place on which you are standing is holy ground.' He said further, 'I am the God of your father, the God of Abraham, the God of Isaac, and the God of Jacob.' And Moses hid his face, for he was afraid to look at God.
>
> Then the LORD said, 'I have observed the misery of my people who are in Egypt; I have heard their cry on account of their taskmasters. Indeed, I know their sufferings, and I have come down to deliver them from the Egyptians, and to bring them up out of that land to a good and broad land, a land flowing with milk and honey, to the country of the Canaanites, the Hittites, the Amorites, the Perizzites, the Hivites, and the Jebusites. The cry of the Israelites has now come to me; I have also seen how the Egyptians oppress them. So come, I will send you to Pharaoh to bring my people, the Israelites, out of Egypt.' But Moses said to God, 'Who am I that I should go to Pharaoh, and bring the Israelites out of Egypt?' He said, 'I will be with you; and this shall be the sign for you that it is I who sent you: when you have brought the people out of Egypt, you shall worship God on this mountain.'

But Moses said to God, 'If I come to the Israelites and say to them, "The God of your ancestors has sent me to you", and they ask me, "What is his name?" what shall I say to them?' God said to Moses, 'I AM WHO I AM.' He said further, 'Thus you shall say to the Israelites, "I AM has sent me to you."' God also said to Moses, 'Thus you shall say to the Israelites, "The LORD, the God of your ancestors, the God of Abraham, the God of Isaac, and the God of Jacob, has sent me to you": This is my name for ever, and this my title for all generations.'   (Exod. 3.1–15)

After hearing the passage, each person takes time to choose a significant word or idea. The passage is read again. People are invited to share their choices. The passage is read once more. What threads emerge?

- Possibly 'I am' – given as God's name;
- Moses does not stand by and watch but responds to God's call;
- How do we respond to God's calling to us?
- What else emerges for you?

Ten-minute break for refreshments.

Revisiting a critical question

What critical question(s) have come to light?

Although yours will be particular to you, as a prompt, here are questions that have occurred for other churches:

- The range of worship you offer.
- Your contact with younger families.
- The possibilities of working with a local school.
- Anxieties about finance.
- Urgent issues of poverty or crime.
- An apparent shortage of 'ministers'.
- How can we contribute to improving pride in this area?
- Is our baptism policy working?
- Matters of justice, e.g. local housing provision, support for asylum seekers.

- Your church's involvement in the wider world.
- The need to redevelop or close a building.

Scripture shows how, when God blesses people and communities, they are invited to recognize their gifts, take the longer view and widen their horizon.

- Consider together how your local church already makes a creative difference to your local community.
- What more might God now be asking of your church in the neighbourhood/world?
- Are you personally now being invited by God to get more practically involved?

In advance of this conversation, consider the following thoughts (on pages 90–2) about being a church of abundance that might open up a renewed sense of vocation.

Food for the journey: God's ways of 'towardness'

Following Jesus is living with the grain of the universe. Christian ethics commends those things that run with the grain of the universe, and amplifies those practices that enrich and enable that life; explicitly or implicitly it critiques those things that run against the grain. Following Jesus means learning to want the limitless things God gives us in Jesus.   (Samuel Wells 2006, p. 5)

Wise ones in every age have let God come towards them and have been willing to let much of their self-centredness be 'burned' away. This vibrant 'towardness' of God is the love that forms the heart of all creation. We can be part of its movement too. God regards us with immense delight and draws us into knowing we are blessed and can share in God's passionate desire for the wholeness of Creation.

Clues to being Church as a wisdom community

In twos and then in the group, consider some of the following statements. Think of ways your church lives in these habits.

- **Living together as God's people in the gift of unity** (Ps. 133.1–3).
  Celebrating difference, held up in prayer, learning God's wisdom and ministering from the Spirit's gifts (Eph. 3.10) – such a church will offer hospitality, live out of God's abundant generosity, and welcome everyone, of any age, at all times and growing as God's people, for ever linked with the name of Jesus Christ (Eph. 1.17–18; 4.1–6).
- **Desiring and learning holiness** (Isa. 6.3; Rev. 4.8).
  To desire holiness is to respond to the call of God to the people of God to be like God (1 Pet. 1.14–16) in goodness and beauty (Ps. 19.7–10). The priority will be the transformation of desire through prayer and worship. Discipleship grows in the movement between accepting the gift and also longing for a life that enacts the love of God in attitude and practice. One of the most trusted signs of having received holiness has been the intercession, 'Come Holy Spirit!'

  A church that is a school for holiness will be one where its people have chosen to let themselves be drawn towards God, rather than to alternative distractions, and to praise in participation through music, words and action, celebrating with all who have gone before and those yet to come.
- **Interconnecting with all who are open to being part of God's ways with the world** (Eph. 1.10; Gen. 12.3).
  Church is its people dispersed and engaged in every aspect of human life and endeavour. This Church, seeking to be an embodiment of the gospel, will not be protected from various patterns of crucifixion but will experience the scandal of resurrection through putting itself where newness needs to emerge to counter evil, disappointment and the damage humans can inflict on one another. Building an open house for creativity, the learning of wisdom, the sharing of God through music, drama, literature, art, economics and politics, is the result of living in praise and eucharistic living. This Church will be keen to connect with people everywhere,

sharing joy, pain and the search for sustainable futures (Gen. 12.1; Luke 9.23).

- **Learning, teaching and being sent out** (Matt. 28.16–20). To follow the Apostles is the gift and calling that combines the exercise of authority with obedience, worship, sending and being sent, being confidently identified with God who is Father, Son and Holy Spirit, passing on faith, welcoming strangers and showing how to be in communion with Jesus (Matt. 25.35, 40).

- This work begins in the sending by the Father of the Son and the Spirit so that in the world churches can do what Jesus did in the power of the Spirit: healing the sick, feeding the hungry, drawing people back into relationship with God, and reconciling people and communities.

  It often means walking towards controversy and complex deliberation for the reinterpretation of faith in ever-new situations. That complexity is opened in the pages of the New Testament where sometimes it is the Spirit who makes Jesus present, sometimes Jesus who makes the Father known and sometimes the Spirit who reveals the Father's word (for example as a dove, when Jesus at his baptism in the Jordan knows more profoundly he is the beloved of the Father – Luke 3.22).

  Such a church will deliberately offer different paths of learning to people and groups, according to need, will be searching for new truth and the Trinitarian God at work and play in the everyday, and will be living faithfully, whatever life sends.

Getting more involved in the local community

If this is what Church can be like, how can we become more like that – and how can we get more involved in our locality or recognize how much we are involved, often invisibly?

- What does this say about our critical question(s)?
- What suggestions come up for changing our way of being Church?

- How can this be fed into the wider Church?
- Who else needs to hear what we are saying here?

Table 1 overleaf should help you collect in one place what the different voices in the group are saying. You might find it helpful, before the group meeting, to draw this table on large sheets of paper.

As you complete the list in Table 1, try to catch yourselves when you're in danger of focusing so much on Church as 'gathered' that you lose sight of the equal calling to be Church 'dispersed', working with God in the world.

Preparing for the next conversation

- What would you like the wider congregation to hear?
- Is there a display area or a sermon slot that could be used for a presentation?
- What support does our companion need?
- What might you say to your friends about being part of this group?
- Read the story of Jacob in Genesis 27 (and the chapters either side if you have time).

Closing prayer

> Loving Father
> help us not to get overloaded by too many projects
> and strategies to serve you.
> Draw us into that same relationship that Jesus shared with you;
> so that we move in your strength, in your direction and your time. **Amen**.

The current fast-paced, knowledge rich, technological age has not satisfied deep hungers for wholeness or positive relatedness to God, self, others and the environment.

(Wimberly and Parker 2012, p. 12)

Table 1   Summarizing how your church is blessed to be a blessing

God's guide to being church	How do we contribute to this through our church?	Where can we see that fresh initiatives could be needed?
1 Sharing life: celebrating difference		
2 Open to God's gifts and actively passing them on		
3 Hospitable, generous and welcoming		
4 Growth: expanding and deepening in discipleship to Jesus		
5 Committed to holiness, in goodness, beauty, word and action		
6 Ready to collaborate with all of good will		
7 Engaged in every aspect of human life and endeavour		

God's guide to being church	How do we contribute to this through our church?	Where can we see that fresh initiatives could be needed?
8 Crossing boundaries to work for change and hope		
9 Outward looking		
10 Engaging with God through: • art • drama • literature • music • economics • politics		
11 Learning, in order to be sent out for 'faith sharing'		
12 Carrying on Jesus' ministry of healing, reconciliation and prophetic challenge		

(Acknowledgments to Colin Gough and the conversation group at Shilbottle, Northumberland)

8 Conversation 4: Blessed to become a blessing

> Conversation is not just about conveying information or sharing emotions, nor just a way of putting ideas into people's heads . . . it is a meeting of minds with different memories and habits. When minds meet they don't just exchange facts; they transform them, reshape them, draw different implications from them, and engage in new trains of thought. Conversation doesn't just reshuffle the cards; it creates new cards.
>
> (Theodore Zeldin, quoted in Lewis et al. 2008, p. 71)

Gathering

- Greet one another, notice who has not arrived and sing or listen to music on CD.
- What has come to mind since we last met?
- Arising out of these conversations, what would we want the wider congregation, or someone we know who isn't part of our church, to know?
- Should we make a display somewhere?
- What is changing in us?
- Read a poem, perhaps 'Dreams and Visions: A Blessing' by Jan Sutch Pickard (2001).

Counting our blessings

What are we good at?

- Cooking, laughing, DIY, parenting, accounting?
- Describe a high point in your church life – when did your faith and/or exercise of your ministry make you feel most alive, engaged, really proud of yourself and your work?
- Without being falsely humble, what can you be proud of in your approach to leadership:

- the unique gifts you bring?
- the team you're part of?
- the contribution of your church to the wider world?

- What are the core values that give life to your church at its best? (For example, that we are equally blessed by God, serving others, keeping people's trust and respect, open to critical friends.)
- What practices or habits demonstrate such claims?

Prayer

Someone leads a prayer arising from the previous conversation.

Food for the journey: turning to God

But now thus says the LORD,
  he who created you, O Jacob,
  he who formed you, O Israel:
Do not fear, for I have redeemed you;
  I have called you by name, you are mine.
When you pass through the waters, I will be with you;
  and through the rivers, they shall not overwhelm you;
when you walk through fire you shall not be burned,
  and the flame shall not consume you.
For I am the LORD your God,
  the Holy One of Israel, your Saviour.
I give Egypt as your ransom,
  Ethiopia and Seba in exchange for you.
Because you are precious in my sight,
  and honoured, and I love you,
I give people in return for you,
  nations in exchange for your life.   (Isa. 43.1–4a)

In this conversation the focus is on God's desire for us to know how deeply we are blessed and our willingness to be reborn in blessing.

The companion steers us through some of the following prompts, allowing for conversation on the way.

Healing and restored relationship

The story of Jacob:

* Isaac and his wife Rebekah have two sons, Esau and Jacob (who was born holding on to his twin Esau heel).
* In Genesis 27 we read how, through a deception, it is Jacob the younger, not his elder brother Esau, who receives the traditional blessing of his father. But as he had 'stolen' what was not his due, he was not really able to receive it as a benefit.
* These ancient narratives were originally handed down by word of mouth. They invite us to recognize ourselves and all families struggling to be faithful to God's call.

In twos and then in the group share:

* any sense in which you, your family or church have not really felt blessed;
* when you had the feeling that you just had to manage without support;
* the way that affected you;
* what difference it makes when we believe we are blessed.

Words may fail us as we try to describe God's love; but God's love will never fail us as we try to bring its brilliance, richness and transformative power to the world around us.

(McGrath 2008, p. 21)

* For much of his life Jacob felt alone. For 20 difficult years he had no sense of being blessed, despite the words his father spoke to him.
* Then Genesis 32 describes Jacob's famous night-long encounter or wrestling with God.

  * Here Jacob finds freedom at last.
  * He realizes for the first time that to know God at the heart of everything is his true goal.
  * He demands that God gives him a real blessing. It changes his life overnight (32.29).

* His struggle with God – described as an angel or a man – leaves him with a limp.

- He had falsely taken his father's blessing by the tradition of putting his hand under his thigh. Now, through being wounded in the same place in his own body, he has discovered healing and the blessing he so much needed.
- Jacob renamed the place where he had wrestled a blessing from God. He called it 'Peny'el', which means 'turn to God'. As dawn broke at the end of that night, although he had been injured, Jacob had a new sense of himself.
- The blessing of God brought a new beginning.
- Consider: **God is either in all things or in nothing**.

Psalm 139 supports our growth in knowing our worth in God's eyes. We could summarize it in a phrase such as, 'Lord, I praise you for the wonder of my being.'

In the group for five minutes and on your own during the coming week, make a time for using this phrase in silence as a thanksgiving to God for the blessing that flows through our lives if we will only allow it.

Holy anger

Jacob had been carrying unspoken anger. He was angry with his father, his brother, his mother, his uncle, his cousins and with God. Until his experience at the Jabbock, he didn't confront others but kept his head down.

'How are you today?' 'Mustn't complain', we say (Job 1.21b).

There's a long tradition among religious people that we should accept our lot and bottle our anger. What makes God angry? For clues, check out in Matthew the Beatitudes (5.1–11), the challenge to any church (25.31–end) and the account of Jesus in the Temple (21.13–14).

How is it possible to be angry with someone as a way of growing in rather than breaking relationship with them?

Finding our place in God's purposes

Scripture shows God blessing small events and particular moments. It also shows that we have to choose to ask for and accept a blessing. It is always available and free but we have to enter into it positively, to be ready.

Seen through God's eyes, every detail of life carries the colour, sound or memory of being created by God for God's purposes, blessed to become a blessing.

In conversation:

* Make a random list of people, places and objects from your experience that carry the 'music' of God's presence and imprint and say why you have chosen them.

To think about for next time

* Is it possible that we have attended church for many years and not really looked to be blessed?
* Is it possible that our churches carry on business as usual with a good reputation, while avoiding the pain of wrestling a true blessing from God?
* How far does this living on the surface affect our ability to be a blessing to others?

Closing prayer

What emerges from the conversation for prayer?

For next time, read Mark 12.12–44 and check other tasks.

Celebration

How will you celebrate the final – *at least for now* – conversation?

Plans for a review gathering

Consider reaping the benefits of ending this series of conversations with a review of the experience and what has changed for individuals or the church. If other groups locally have been working through the conversations, why not share with them. The companions could devise and support structured processes, and the outcomes could be made known to the local church(es) in a presentation of some kind.

9 Conversation 5: There is more than enough!

Blessing is a birth, and makes it possible to give birth to a blessing.

(Basset 2007, p. 250)

Gathering

- The group gathers and shares news and reflections since the last conversation.
- What is emerging for you about being blessed in order to become a blessing?

Prayer

The group shares prayer, a poem, food, a picture; a song is sung or music played.

Blessed to go!

From the last conversation:

- Consider alone, then share a random list of people, places and objects from your experience that carry the 'music' of God's blessing, presence and imprint.
- Tell one another why you have chosen them.
- What are they are saying to you about who God is?

Continuing the group conversation, trust one another as far as you can with your response to these questions:

- How far are we ready to accept that we are truly blessed – 'God's beloved'?
- Can this go beyond words?
- What are the feelings that go with this?

Let's recall one of the key New Testament passages that reminds us that we belong to a community rooted in the belief in God's unconditional love for us:

> In those days Jesus came from Nazareth of Galilee and was baptized by John in the Jordan. And just as he was coming up out of the water, he saw the heavens torn apart and the Spirit descending like a dove on him. And a voice came from heaven, 'You are my Son, the Beloved; with you I am well pleased.'
>
> (Mark 1.9–11)

By now the group will be perfectly capable of reading this text together and letting God speak through it. Only if you need them, some of the following pointers may be helpful:

- Jesus invites us to join him in knowing we are daughters and sons of God the Father.
- Scripture shows God coming close in small events and particular moments.
- Scripture also shows that we have to choose to step into the invitation – to ask for and accept blessing.
- Blessing is what God constantly offers, but we have to enter into it and be ready for what may follow.

The invitation of these conversations is to:

- let ourselves be more and more drawn into knowing God's desire to share life with us;
- become Church increasingly known for our generosity, as called by name, loved, abundant, forgiven, singing, glorifying, celebrating, worshipping;
- and so pray to become more willing to share in God's work in the world.

Jesus: sign of God's abundance

This Scripture passage is read by several voices, followed by a silence and an exchange of responses.

> The apostles gathered around Jesus, and told him all that they had done and taught. He said to them, 'Come away to a deserted

place all by yourselves and rest a while.' For many were coming and going, and they had no leisure even to eat. And they went away in the boat to a deserted place by themselves. Now many saw them going and recognized them, and they hurried there on foot from all the towns and arrived ahead of them. As he went ashore, he saw a great crowd; and he had compassion for them, because they were like sheep without a shepherd; and he began to teach them many things. When it grew late, his disciples came to him and said, 'This is a deserted place, and the hour is now very late; send them away so that they may go into the surrounding country and villages and buy something for themselves to eat.' But he answered them, 'You give them something to eat.' They said to him, 'Are we to go and buy two hundred denarii worth of bread, and give it to them to eat?' And he said to them, 'How many loaves have you? Go and see.' When they had found out, they said, 'Five, and two fish.' Then he ordered them to get all the people to sit down in groups on the green grass. So they sat down in groups of hundreds and of fifties. Taking the five loaves and the two fish, he looked up to heaven, and blessed and broke the loaves, and gave them to his disciples to set before the people; and he divided the two fish among them all. And all ate and were filled; and they took up twelve baskets full of broken pieces and of the fish. Those who had eaten the loaves numbered five thousand men.   (Mark 6.30–44)

If the group needs prompts for conversation, the following are ways of challenging our church to recognize that beyond the market economy of sending people to the shops to buy food, Jesus invites his disciples to open their eyes to the greater reality of having all that we need to feed others:

- Jesus' miracles show that when we bless God for God's sake, anything can happen. Scripture is brimming over with examples of this basic challenge: **know you are blessed in order to become a blessing**.
- Where do we think we stand? With Jesus or with the disciples?
- Week by week, churches come together in the Eucharist (Holy Communion, Mass). With Christians of all ages and

all places, we celebrate God's amazing blessings and then are sent away to be reckless blessings to others.

- How does this fit with your experience?
- Do you get too busy with church matters and so miss a deeper experience?
- Do you sometimes just turn up, not expecting much?
- What could you do about this?

Food for the journey: taking, blessing, breaking and sharing

Read again Mark 6.30–44 and then keep a silence – choose a word or phrase to share.

Mark's Gospel addresses followers of Jesus who have a sense of inadequacy. Even when in Jesus we are shown God's abundance, we live in doubt.

- Mark tells how huge crowds followed Jesus and his disciples, wherever they went.
- He taught them to know the true God in stories from everyday life. These were often stories that needed to be thought about over a long period. Each time we read them, a new meaning may appear.
- Showing what God's love is like (even when he was tired from preaching and healing), Jesus fed them all. At his core was the desire for their lives to be turned around through experiencing God – moving towards them in overwhelming generosity.
- Jesus used ordinary food as a window into God, a sacramental sign of God's loving kindness.

> *Taking* the five loaves and the two fish, he looked up to heaven, and *blessed* and *broke* the loaves, and *gave* them to his disciples to set before the people.   (Mark 6.41a)

These words would be as familiar to Mark's hearers as they are to us. They are the four key actions of the Eucharist: Jesus *took*, *blessed*, *broke* and *shared* the ordinary stuff of life (fish and loaves), and through blessing God he transformed them into God's self-giving generosity. All had everything they needed.

Mark doesn't explain what happened – he lets the miracle stand in its own right. We're invited to listen and watch and be awed by God's capacity to create abundance.

Reflection

What can we learn here, personally and as churches, about the overflowing power of God?

In the world where Jesus is Lord, we need not be anxious about running out or not having enough.

Prayer

Say together slowly:

> Jesus, we want to overturn our sense of
> scarcity, anxiety, fearfulness and greed.
> We are sorry to be so slow to believe.
> We don't get that you are at work
> in the everyday world of bread and food and money.
> We don't get that you, Jesus, are the Lord who
> presides over the whole of our lives.
> We don't get that when you are among us
> there is always more than we need or can imagine.
> Overcome our slowness.
> Help us to unlearn our habits of scarcity.
> Let the world see your abundance.
> Begin with us,
> so that the world may recognize how
> you make everything different.
> Help us to act as if we knew this to be true. **Amen**.
> (With glad acknowledgment to the style of Walter
> Brueggemann's prayers against the myth of scarcity
> and celebrating abundance – Brueggemann 2003)

Revisiting a critical question

- In relation to your critical question, revisit earlier conversations about how your being blessed leads on to being a blessing to others.

- What is the blessing you have to share?
- How could that make a difference to the local neighbourhood?
- How could it help you to address the critical question your church currently faces?

Review

- What have you learnt about God?
- What have you learnt about your church, neighbourhood and yourself?
- What would be a positive outcome of this series of conversations?

Closing prayer

- A form of mutual blessing planned beforehand? 'May the Lord bless you deeply'
- A blessing of your neighbourhood?
- Thanks!

Celebration

Saying farewell – food and drink!

Plans for a review gathering (companion and host with others)

- What was your response to the critical question?
- How did the question change?
- How did asking the question change you?
- How will you report your findings to your church council and leaders?

The LORD bless you and keep you;
the LORD make his face to shine upon you, and be gracious to you;
the LORD lift up his countenance upon you, and give you peace.
(Num. 6.24–26)

In planning to review the conversations, more detailed questions might be:

1 Can you evaluate the process in terms of who stayed in the groups and who left, and how the roles of host and companion worked for everyone?
2 What does it mean to perceive your church(es) as a blessing to the area? What have you learnt of the cries of joy and pain in your neighbourhood? How can you be an influence locally?
3 To what extent is your church motivated to be a blessing to others? How would you like others to speak of you?
4 To what extent could your premises and property be further released into public life? What changes would be required – in your self-understanding and practices?
5 Who are you called to love and to work with?

10 Creative development: examples of taking the conversations further

> While book knowledge is important and necessary, it is the experience of real life, both favourable and challenging, and reflection on those experiences, that are exceedingly helpful in our formation of wisdom.
>
> (Wimberly and Parker 2012, p. 38)

The power of conversation

Those churches that have 'road-tested' these conversations have given valuable feedback on their experiences of these encounters and the power of conversation. Some have obviously experienced a release of new energy through the invitation to talk openly about blessing.

Here are some of the comments to emerge from those who have been companions to conversation groups:

- 'The conversational approach has proved to be transformative and the groups seem to be getting the hang of it, and are meeting each other at a different level than in the groups they are more accustomed to. Some of the sharing has been quite personal.'
- 'Our group was moved through affirming and being affirmed. Mutual appreciation is building confidence and competence in us.'
- 'A lot has changed personally for me as a result of taking part in these conversations.'
- 'We most certainly felt this was a helpful way to change our way of being together, and we hope to introduce this more widely in our church.'

Generally there is a sense that taking part in conversation is more than passing on information, sharing feelings or trying to persuade people to do something.

What did emerge, though, was the vital need for groups to take the basic structures offered here and remake them to fit their particular circumstances. To see how some churches expanded on the materials in the book may stimulate your church to add to, adapt and use it in your situation.

Conversations on texts

Jesus shows God's abundance

The congregation of Bolton Priory in Yorkshire held a weekly Bible study in parallel to the conversations, using some of the same scriptural passages. Not everyone took part in both events. Simon Cowling, the rector, describes here the fourth in a series of five. It is based on Mark 6.30–44, which was quoted in full in Chapter 9 (see page 102).

A harvest poem

> We bring our gifts:
> The first-fruits of our labour,
> or perhaps the spare we do not need,
> (an offering to mitigate against our greed).
> To the church we bring them,
> and into the hands of Christ we place them,
> and we say, 'Take this,
> and do with it some miracle:
> Turn water into wine again,
> or multiply my loaves and fish
> to feed a crowd again.'
> And Jesus takes them from our hand,
> this fruit of the ocean, this product of the land,
> and blesses them, accepting back
> what always was the Lord's.
> Our gifts will fill the lack
> of hungry people,
> putting flesh on words
> of charity, and making folk

in our small corner of the world
more equal.
We know there is enough for everyone.
But once the leftovers are gone –
taken to the homeless, hungry poor –
what of those twelve empty baskets standing idly by?
Can there yet be more
that we can ask our Lord to multiply?
Into those baskets therefore let us place ourselves,
those parts of us that need transforming,
grace and strength and healing,
the gifts in us that need to be increased and shared
with a greater generosity than we may be prepared
to offer on our own account.
For we are God's rich and splendid bounty,
seeds, sown and scattered by the Lord in every place.
the human race:
the crowning glory
of the ever-evolving creation story.
We thank the Lord
that he does not just separate wheat from tare,
but takes our very best
then turns us into far more than we are.

> (Ally Barrett, <https://reverendally.wordpress.
> com/poems>)

Personal reflection

Slowly read the Scripture text again on your own. Without looking for any 'right' answers, reflect on some of these questions:

- Where is your attention drawn?
- What do you notice with fresh clarity?
- What surprises or challenges you?
- If there were a New Testament scholar in the room, what questions would you ask?
- What challenges do you think this passage might pose for the Bolton Priory community?
- How might the Bolton Priory community respond?

Group reflection

We listen, without interruption, as each person offers the fruit of their reflection. We have a general discussion on the passage, informed by the reflections we have heard. We end with Night Prayer from *Common Worship*. We found this helpful for two reasons. First, because it was the same each week it provided a unifying thread for the participants (rather like that wonderful sky that unites Frank Brangwyn's mosaics of the life of St Aidan in St Aidan's Church in Harehills, Leeds). Second, it allowed the opportunity to reflect on the biblical passage used in the *lectio divina* in a – gently – liturgical context, so helping people to see that Scripture affects us in different ways, depending on context.

Sharing food and Eucharist

Hope Lutheran Church, Selden, New York, added to each of the conversations a shared meal. Pastor Richard Hill writes:

> The group starts out with a 15-minute Lenten Table Eucharist, which sets the stage for the conversation that follows. We use a small chalice and paten that I got when I visited Durham Cathedral. We also choose songs to draw out the theme of the conversations. The eucharistic rite is found on: <http://sicutlocutusest. com/2013/02/07/a-communion-liturgy-for-lent>. I like the way the Communion Service we are using leads into the conversations. Our Gospel reading was the Beatitudes and since we are having 'table communion' in the fellowship hall after having shared a meal together, there is a positive attitude toward being a blessing to others that is growing among us.

Interpreting the conversations

Louise Taylor-Kenyon, parish priest of Embsay with Eastby, writes:

> Having been asked to 'road-test' the book with a group in our local churches, I decided to offer this material for study in Lent this year. The context is a small semi-rural self-confident parish,

with a tradition of occasional time-limited, small-group sessions, usually five or six weekly sessions two or three times a year. These are often shared with the Methodist chapel in the village but for this occasion we did this on our own as I felt that the 'critical question' that emerged would be different if we shared this together.

I was helped by the emphasis on inclusivity, which begins before the group meets by asking for preferences for time and day, valuing the commitment that people are prepared to make. Formerly, as a curate this was something I used to do, but with increased workload I have lost the habit of doing so, and it was good to be prompted to do so again. I used this as an opportunity to explain to the congregation that these were *conversations*, intentionally setting up a space where everyone's voice could be heard, where prior knowledge was less important than a willingness to participate.

I found it hard to recruit a companion who I felt would 'get' the way the conversations would work, so as I am used to facilitating small groups and am confident about managing conversations, I decided to become the companion myself. As far as the process was concerned I think this worked well, but I was surprised by the way I was torn between my need to continue to act as a pastor and the needs of managing the group. For example, I don't have a problem with making sure that everyone has a chance to contribute and encouraging people who dominate to let others have space, but I found myself needing to validate someone who was getting off the point rather than simply asking them if they thought the point they were making was relevant.

On the other hand, because the process itself was very successful, after the second week I was able to sit lightly to this as other people in the group asked that question anyway, or brought the conversation back on track themselves. In other words, the process itself allowed the group to take responsibility.

I decided to adapt the material in Part 2 extensively, as after reading the whole book through, and rereading the conversations material, I felt that it would take more time than we had available each week to cover everything. This is almost inevitable!

I gave each week a title and produced a small handout – A4 landscape, double-sided, folded to make an A5 booklet – with the material that we would need, the crucial questions I would ask and something to think about for the following week. Although this might seem time-consuming, I never saw Robin's book as an off-the-peg resource, and I knew I would need to spend time in preparation, so this was simply a way of codifying the ideas I had and sharing them in an accessible way. As I read through each week's conversation section, I made my own notes, incorporating any insights from the previous conversation, and allocated a time to each section, to make sure that as far as possible we completed the material each week. Inevitably this did not always work, but I was able to skip sections or ask people to look at them during the week, so that each conversation was a whole and was not cut short in the middle.

I think this flexibility was really important, *as it allowed us to spend time exploring what really mattered to this specific group in this specific context, rather than feeling that we had to talk about everything.* I used quotes and prayers that are included in the text of the five conversations, as well as other prayers that I felt were relevant. Although the group didn't have the complete text of the conversations, I usually printed out the *lectio divina* passage provided in each conversation so that we all had access to it. Of course people bring Bibles, but it is easier to pinpoint specific words and phrases if everyone has the same text in front of them.

A total of 12 people, including myself, took part in the five weeks of conversations. This is from a regular congregation of 35–40, an electoral roll of 68. One person was on placement with us from anther church. I had intended to hand over 'companionship' to another member of the group after three weeks but realized that without having that person as an apprentice from the very beginning it would be difficult to do as people had got so involved in the conversation process that it would be difficult for anyone to withdraw from being a participant.

The people who took part were a new 'grouping', in that they had not met in this particular configuration before but they all knew each other to varying degrees. The conversations allowed an atmosphere of trust to develop very quickly, within which people asked difficult and deeply felt questions, shared life experiences at an extraordinary level of painfulness and depth, were silent together, laughed and talked together and discovered a greater awareness of being blessed, of where God came in their lives and of joy in their church community. On several occasions I had to leave to collect children as the sessions overran, and each time I came back expecting to find that everyone had gone, only to find that they were still talking avidly.

Two critical themes emerged, both of which have several sub-questions or suggestions as to how they might be met or develop. One was based on 'How do we share our blessings with our community?', which led to a whole string of suggestions about what we might do, and further questions. It took a while to get beyond the idea that this was about getting people into church, but once we did, *a torrent of creativity and energy was released.*

The other theme was about how we find the language we need to tell people about the treasure that we possess in our faith, and exposed a real sense of being poorly equipped to *talk* about faith. Given that many people in this group are visibly living their faith on a day-to-day basis, it was interesting and rather disconcerting to find how diffident they feel about expressing it – but it was also important to have this question aired so that the group members discovered that they were not alone in this. In a church that has been quite content with itself, with a culture of simply expecting people to come to faith if they come to church or come to an explorers group, just acknowledging that talking about faith outside church is desirable is a big step – and one that will not necessarily be shared by everyone in the congregation.

These three examples illustrate very well how this whole venture into being more present in church conversations is vital and holds much potential, provided people have a measure of safety for being more vulnerable with one another. They also demonstrate how this is not an off-the-peg course but an introduction to travel that requires forethought as well as openness to what comes. These comments also underwrite my sense that the companion has to find a confident enough place to steer the group but also to let God be God.

PART 3

INTEGRATING A CONVERSATIONAL APPROACH TO CHURCH DEVELOPMENT

11 Transformational conversation: maintaining the approach

Is it not a paradox that the chief practical function of so many religious organizations is to protect people from religious experience? Are they afraid the faithful might go off the reservation?

(Hollis 2013, p. 25)

Maintaining the spirit of enquiry

My hope is that this brief introduction to the benefits of Participatory Action Research, linked with the deep Jewish/Christian tradition of blessing, may support churches to learn intimacy and to address problems in fresh ways. In his weekly column in *The Guardian*, Giles Fraser takes the view that the Church of England is 'holding up pretty well in an adverse market' (15 November 2014, p. 40). He argues that the hunger that churches can meet will never go away despite the persuasions of atheists:

> Churchgoing is about the solidarity of sitting in the same pew, being involved in the same liturgy, trying to get on with people with whom you don't have anything in common. We have survived every conceivable war, crisis, scandal, collapse and disillusionment. OK, we may not have the money to keep the heating on all the time. But don't expect the 'for sale' sign to go up anytime soon. (Ibid.)

His position resonates with that of the sociologist of religion Alan Billings (theological educator and Police Commissioner for South Yorkshire), who in the same week, at the 2014 National Shared Ministry Conference held in Manchester, revalued an albeit more modest Anglican presence as sustainer, through thick and mostly thin, of continuity and tradition in local neighbourhoods. Respecting the subtle modes of how people are able to belong, attend and believe is, he suggests, a vital characteristic of Christian practice.

I would differ with him in his optimism that the demise of the Welfare State will gradually bring a return of popular appreciation of the Anglican way of doing Church, though it may well be that as with valuing food banks and making up the pastoral care that for the second half of the twentieth century was subsumed into the Welfare State, churches find a renewed role.

The sustained proposal of this book is that churches that reinvent themselves in the coming decades will have moved on from the binary poles of either being unconcerned about membership or of purposefully seeking a gathered homogeneity. Churches need to be forming disciples, not members, both in the intensity of God's call and in the extensity of seeking to work with God in the public square. To focus on membership is to create churches of those whose focus is largely on having their apparent needs met by others commissioned as 'ministering' agents.

The invitation of the Spirit now seems to be to recognize that for all Christians, discipleship is the essential bedrock of being Church. The calling to particular ministries, essential as that may be, is secondary to being an equal participant in the community of God's beloved. In this post-Christendom period, to avoid the polarities of being totally open with no centre or sharply centred with firm boundaries, missional churches reflect the abundance of God by holding in tension a purposeful, open and welcoming church. The calling to particular ministries, essential as that may be, is secondary to being an equal participant in the community of God's beloved. In Part 3 of the book my intention is to persuade churches to choose, shape and hold many formative conversations on themes that will help them to discover fresh language, metaphors and direction. I have selected a variety of real conversations by way of encouragement. I appreciate the insight of Anthony B. Robinson, who sets out a comprehensive list of strategic topics for conversation 'about what God is up to in our time and how we are called to respond'. His list includes:

1 'It's Not About You.'
2 'And Yet . . . It *Is* About You.'
3 'A New Heart (made up of four vessels: evangelism, worship, Scripture and theology).'

4 'Who Shall Lead Them?'
5 'Why Are We Here?'
6 'Write the Vision.'   (Robinson 2008, pp. 12–14)

God as our deepest source

The transformational conversations on blessing included here provide a framework that invites churches to foster greater self-knowledge, companionship, sense of resourcefulness and openness to God, together with a prophetic voice, compassion for society, spirit of enquiry and capacity for embracing diversity.

Many parish clergy recognize their role as attempting to support Christians in their mostly dispersed ministry and witness in the extensiveness of God's world. Yet the increasing ratio between congregations and stipendiary clergy frustrates these hopes. Local churches need the wider support gained by working across missional or ministry areas, not in competition but in partnership. In dioceses and regions there are often strategic plans for keeping the old system going or even making some adjustments.

But as followers of the crucified Christ, churches can only be 'fixed' in ways that tell the story of a future opened by the Spirit through the forsakenness of the Father's Son at Golgotha. In the Church of England nationally the Archbishop's Council published a report, *Developing Discipleship*, in which the Bishop of Sheffield, Stephen Croft, called for a revised form of the catechism and a theological conversation on discipleship and ministry (see *Church Times* of 16 January 2015 and the continuing media conversations). Similarly the Roman Catholic Diocese of Hexham, alert to the many threats to its previous ways of functioning, has been inspired by Pope Francis' Apostolic Exhortation of 2013. Inviting churches to move beyond the attitude 'We've always done it this way', Pope Francis urges them to be fearless and courageous – to face the need to be 'in the task of rethinking the goals, structure, style and methods of evangelization in their respective communities' (*Evangelii Gaudium*, 33). So every parish in the Diocese of Hexham is now being supported to focus on restructuring, recognizing the blessing of the Holy Spirit and the urgent need for clergy and people to talk to and pray with one another: 'The Success of Forward

Together in Hope depends on all of us playing our part and thinking beyond existing boundaries . . . join the journey of renewal for our diocese by praying and offering of your skills and talents' (Fr Jim O'Keefe and Tony Sacco, development officers, autumn 2014). Self-evaluation by local churches has been a key starting place. At the time of completing this research, unique data packs have been distributed to parishes in the Hexham Diocese. The figures for Fr David's parishes reveal plummeting statistics of mass attendance between 1985 and 2014. A detailed questionnaire provides a framework for each parish community in the diocese to explore its vitality and future direction. The material emphasizes the importance of a combination of prayer, consultation and reflection with a systematic recording of the outcomes of deliberations (<hope@diocesehn.org.uk>). As with all such painstaking surveys of the realities of church life, this is a first courageous step.

For radical innovation to be successful requires a fundamental transformation of the energy and expectations of involvement of previously passive congregations. Fr David remains buoyant that through conversations and the power of the Holy Spirit, a sea change will be possible. A new initiative for several historic churches of different denominations in Darlington to support each other in finding vehicles for change adds to his sense of hope for a genuine exodus, 'the journey of each Christian soul and the entire Church, the decisive turning of our lives towards the Father' (Pope Francis, *Letter for Vocations Sunday 2015*).

Lectio divina: dynamic corporate Bible study

In my research project I have found that one of the most helpful elements in advocating this approach to being Church has been doing *lectio divina* with groups ranging in size from just three or four people to over 30. I think this off-centring approach to Scripture, faith and God symbolizes the entire approach. It links personal and corporate reflection on Scripture and God in all things; it leaves no one out because it invites everyone to communicate whatever and whenever they can.

The purpose of *lectio* is to create relationship – with God and therefore with everyone and everything. It nurtures friendship and can include silence, inquiry, tears and bursts of laughter. Its corporate practice builds confidence and invites participants to move from mere acquaintance to ever deeper levels of *presence*.

The aim of Appreciative Inquiry conversations, rooted in blessing, is to foster a culture of respect as a way of releasing growth and maturity in churches. Awareness and mindfulness are much needed for authentic living in a time of uncertainty and anxiety for church communities. They act as a counterbalance to attempts to ignore the problems, or to try to fix them mechanically or by restructuring dioceses.

These conversations suggest a way of being Church that allows for stopping and truly listening – to God, to our neighbourhoods, to one another. There is always the danger that, with no idea where we are going, we have no time to reflect or find out. The form of Church that God is creating in our present time is still unclear. Often we seem to be going backwards. But in honest and open conversation we have humble indicators that the people of the world are not without God's love. There persists an ever-present surplus of goodness, truth and beauty to enrich the world's life.

The Oxford University mindfulness centre (<www.oxfordmindfulness. org>) describes itself as an international centre of excellence within Oxford University's Department of Psychiatry that works with partners around the world to prevent depression and enhance human potential through the therapeutic use of mindfulness. Here is a key agency within a growing global movement that focuses on taking account of emotions, thoughts and sensations together, rather than in compartments. Taking time for conversation and for corporate silence can help churches to remain calm but focused, even when they have to accept that the future cannot be a repetition of what was familiar in the past. This handbook aims to offer simple structures for this to become a way of life, a deliberate way of working that combines activity with consideration.

The themes of blessing and wisdom combine and give respect to the different ways that people and communities learn. Letting God be God and praising God for God's own sake allows everyone to take responsibility in some way for curating a space where all may encounter God and discover the pathway to follow.

My own experience of developing this approach through the willingness of church communities to trust leads me to advocate the priorities of listening, noticing, respecting, thanking, receiving, waiting and being present, as well as guarding, preventing harm, standing up to manipulation, resisting the abuse of power and believing that each day we begin in God's blessing.

At the heart of these developments lies the unresolved dilemma of how far churches are literally all God's responsive people, resourced in mission by Scripture, Eucharist, prayer, study, leaders and the ordained, or whether in the end we believe being Church is essentially the work of a reducing number of clergy with 'support' from a largely receptive laity.

The latter view is far from dead. I happened to be walking beyond two young ordinands who were talking loudly. 'I like the way we're being trained for ordination. It's so good that the course is rooted in the practical so much.' 'And I think it's so helpful that we're told that to be "good enough" is fine. We don't want to get burnt out like so many do.' This seems very loving on the part of their tutors. But it appears to me still to be working from the understanding that the work of being Church is just about equivalent to the amount of work that can be accomplished by an overstretched priest in a multi-church setting.

The urgent need for companions in conversation

A vital task for those preparing clergy and other leaders today is to learn how to develop and use processes that release the energy of the whole Church. As we have seen, this goes beyond knowledge garnered from teachers and books. In this third part I conclude with some worked examples of 'conversations'. They have all been road-tested several times and they rely on the agility of the facilitator to 'play' them as the moment decrees. These are not blueprints but are designed to encourage you to take up this work for yourself in ways that work for you. The list of recommended books suggests very practical as well as imaginative resources that have helped me to learn how to devise creative conversations. These reported experiences may, I hope, stimulate you to find the benefits and the facility for dreaming, designing and delivering group process in churches.

Participation in society and in the worship and movement of the local church seems to be a Spirit-led antidote to hierarchical churches that keep themselves pure from the world. These conversations remind me that before such transition towards lay involvement in mission and ministry can take central place in churches there needs to be both humility and respect. *Lectio divina* reminds conversation groups to believe they have been given a gift, a sense of being blessed deeply by God, through praying to the Holy Spirit.

In conversations on blessing we are listening to one another and to Scripture and through them both we are listening to God. So the planned structure of a conversation may well be necessary at first to keep the group accountable to their church and to its participants. For church communities the real challenge of *lectio*, as of conversations on blessing, is gradually to move beyond the externals of who we are as 'church' towards finding who God is calling us to be here and now. Much has been written on this for individual Christians but the focus in this book is on developing authentic expressions of Church. Like people, churches can fortify ourselves with pride in the past or music or the architecture that houses us. Now is not the time to be a great, wealthy, or successful church.

Suppose, instead, we let go of our church's reputation and self-esteem and pray to be known as Moses was known, with a transfigured face through letting God be God. The Trinity of unconditional and flowing blessing invites us to see who we are called to become and what we are capable of becoming – both blessed and a blessing to others – in the degree that we are willing to receive it. God gives us the perfect freedom to resist or to surrender to transformation. My prayer is that you will sense both the peace and the urgency in being called to live in blessing. Paradoxically, just when we think we have got hold of God's word to us – to be consoled or to be consolers – there is something new for us to learn. May you continue to develop practices of listening to one another, to the world and to God, and find courage to continue the work which the Holy Spirit has already begun.

The chapters that follow describe a range of case studies and conversational workshop outlines that I have developed for particular situations. For many readers these processes will be very familiar, but for those who are drawn to this approach but have little experience, I have deliberately shown the detailed working and timings as a springboard for your own inventiveness. My intention is to inspire readers, using their own gifts and opportunities, to continue developing this conversational approach to corporate change.

12   Re-visioning a church through conversation

> The Church also seeks to be a blessing through acts of goodness. Unlike most human communities, the Church's life focuses not on itself, but on those who not belong. It is a community defined by its mission to be a means of blessing.
>
> (Tomlin 2014, p. 105)

Mission Action Planning

The rector, Jill Perrett, and church council (PCC) of the parish of St Peter's, Addingham, a village in West Yorkshire, began a process for renewing their vision. The rector spends one third of her time as an officer in the diocese for clergy ministerial development.

As companion, I met with the rector, who later invited me to a meeting of the PCC. I asked them to be prepared to describe to me the village that is the setting for their church.

At the council meeting we focused on questions about the life of the village, such as:

- How long have you lived here?
- What are you proud of?
- What hinders the life of the village?
- What do you need more of?

Several weeks later I met with a team that the PCC had set up to plan an 'away day' as a way of taking forward the process of re-visioning. In conversation we arrived at five key questions across a wide range of issues for St Peter's mission.

It was agreed that, as an essential part of the away day, members of the planning team would invite members of the congregation to attend a small group meeting. Each group would consider one of the five questions. These group responses would be presented at the away day as a springboard for further conversation.

Appreciative questions

The five questions I originally suggested for consideration by groups before the away day were as follows. Each has several sub-questions:

Group 1: To what end?

(a) What is the final purpose of St Peter's? What is our 'core business'? Read Matthew 5.1–16 and Mark 2.1–12.
(b) Given the answer to (a), consider no more than five core values that would assist St Peter's to reach its stated aim.
(c) List no more than three habits or practices by which you could test whether these values were being lived out.

Group 2: Across the generations

(a) Do you believe that St Peter's exists to serve people of all ages? Is that a core value?
(b) What practices are in place to demonstrate this?
(c) What further practices need to be developed?
(d) What existing practices may actually hinder the development of this value?
(e) Can you think of any words of Jesus to illuminate this issue?

Group 3: Listening to those on the edge

'Those who are not against us are for us' (Jesus); 'the Church is the one organization that exists for the sake of those who do not belong' (attributed to Archbishop William Temple).

(a) In Addingham, which are the groups of people who might well by attracted by God or even by the parish church's stated purpose but at present cannot connect with 'church'?
(b) Have you personal contact with those whose 'culture' seems not to fit with church culture?
(c) The Church of England website and many others carry numerous references to fresh expressions of Church and new forms of Church, such as 'new monasticism'.

(d) What ways might emerge in Addingham for the parish church to meet in several radically different styles that supported each other?

(e) What scriptural images or narratives come to mind on this topic?

Group 4: A presiding ministry

(a) What does Paul mean by his remark in Romans 12.5, 'For as in one body we have many members, and not all the members have the same function, so we, who are many, are one body in Christ, and *individually we are members one of another.*' How far down this road have we travelled?

(b) Consider that baptism gives us gifts for sharing so that, in different ways, all can contribute to the forming and working of Church. At different stages in life our responsibilities will vary.

(c) Consider how 'church' is a collaborative task – to serve God's mission to bring healing and wholeness to the world – in which the priest and other leaders 'preside'. How would you prioritize what is needed *uniquely* from the role of the rector and the team of wardens and other key officials?

Group 5: Church as a 'learning community'

(a) Consider that as 'church' (*thought of as a verb rather than a noun*) we are mostly dispersed in everyday matters and sometimes gather for worship or to take decisions.

(b) What kinds of life-long learning would build up the congregation as followers of Christ for the sake of God's kingdom as defined, say, in Matthew 25 (especially from verse 31)?

A member of the planning team, in response to comments from some participants, agreed to present a simplified version of the questions. They were then used in this revised form:

Question 1: What is St Peter's for?

* In other words, what is our ultimate purpose?
* List no more than three things that we do at St Peter's by which we could test whether we are achieving our purpose.

Question 2: For all ages?

- We believe that St Peter's exists to serve people of all ages, but our congregation does not fully reflect this:

  - What things do we do that demonstrate our commitment to all ages?
  - What else needs to be developed?
  - What do we currently do that might hinder St Peter's service to people of all ages?

Question 3: Emerging church?

- In Addingham, can we identify groups of people who might well be attracted by God but at present cannot connect with 'church'?
- There is much talk about 'fresh expressions' of church, such as messy church, hands on church, cafe church. What ways could emerge in Addingham for the parish church to meet in several radically different styles that reflect the differing ways people feel appropriate to express their faith?

Question 4: A collaborative ministry?

- What progress has St Peter's made in involving lay members of the congregation in its ministry?
- What is the next step in your opinion?
- What do you regard as uniquely the role of the rector, other clergy and Readers?

Question 5: What do we need to learn?

- What opportunities for learning and development have members of the group found most helpful on their Christian journey? If St Peter's is to continue developing the involvement of the laity in mission and ministry, what learning opportunities would be helpful? For example, should there be available at parish, deanery or diocesan level more seminars, house group programmes, sermons, lectures, courses, action learning and so on, and on what topics?

After the five groups had discussed the questions, I met again with the planning team at the proposed away-day venue, a few miles from the parish. There we reviewed the various spaces and my suggested outline for the day.

Away day: practical arrangements

There was a printed-out 'script' for the day for myself as companion and the leadership team. Forty participants were expected, including some children (who would mostly spend time in another room). A large, oblong, well-lit working-room was laid out with tables arranged like spokes of a wheel, each accommodating five or six people. Participants were given a handout with a brief outline of events. Worship information and presentations were shown on PowerPoint on two screens, so that everyone could see them.

In the briefing notes, the leadership team was reminded that this was to be the first of a series of conversations designed to stimulate the renewal of the vision, values and practices of St Peter's, Addingham. Central to these conversations is a growing willingness for all involved to be *present* to God, one another, society and the whole creation. Such presence in conversation can lead to:

* a deepening spirit of mutual affirmation, arising from gratitude;
* a willingness to lament at the world's pain;
* a renewed understanding of faith;
* the discovery of new possibilities;
* accessing fresh energy for seeing old 'problems' in a new light.

These don't come in a neat linear way but unpredictably. The task is to take unhurried time, over the coming months, to face the reality of our church, within the wider Church and God's mission in the world. This will lead to discernment of a future direction of travel together, within God's purposes, through the particular and connected calling of all. For those on the planning team, a priority will be to encourage others to recognize their valued part in this 'beloved community'.

Away day: purpose

The planning team had agreed the purpose that, through conversations, St Peter's would move to a culture of Action Planning. This would include such tasks as expanding the age profile of the congregation, growing maturity in discipleship, involving more people in ministry and reminding everyone how much they were valued. In scriptural terms, it was to know themselves as 'a beloved community that blesses others'. They noted that in many parts of the Church of England the concept of Mission Action Planning had become a way of identifying this approach.

Away day: process for the morning session

(Note: each part of the programme was allocated a rough time slot so that the whole process could be completed on time, with due attention to each part. I have not included the timings here (*or in the following chapters*), so that those making use of these outlines can make their own decisions on them. My experience suggests that clarity about this is vital, even if circumstances lead you to make adjustments in response to what emerges in the conversations.)

Stage 1: Introduction

The group work undertaken in recent weeks is the basis from which we begin.

- The rector and a warden welcome everyone and then Robin as 'companion'.
- Robin responds briefly.
- Housekeeping notices.
- The purpose of the day and commitment to it is briefly expressed by a warden.
- The rector, recognizing the presence of the young ones, leads a prayer.
- A teenager, remaining with the adult group, reads a prayer for pilgrims.

Stage 2: Who are we?

At each table, all present briefly introduce themselves, in turn saying their names. As they tell the group their name, the host invites them to add something particular about 'What you hope for today or why you love being alive or being a Christian or what makes your heart sing.' (NB This is a short exercise in listening, not a discussion!)

Speaking to the whole room, Robin, as companion, briefly reinforces the purpose of the conversation and emphasizes the need to commit to confidentiality – 'We may take away anything we have learnt today except what we have learnt about others.'

Stage 3: Dynamic Bible study – abiding in God's love

From the centre of the room, someone reads this passage slowly:

> As the Father has loved me,
> So I have loved you; abide in my love.
>
> If you keep my commandments,
> you will abide in my love,
> just as I have kept my Father's commandments
> and abide in his love.
>
> I have said these things to you
> so that my joy may be in you,
> and that your joy may be complete.
>
> I do not call you servants any longer,
> because the servant does not know what the
> master is doing;
> but I have called you friends,
> because I have made known to you everything
> that I have heard from my Father.   (John 15.9–11, 15)

In a time of quiet, Robin invites everyone on each table to pick a word that stands out especially. After a few minutes we are invited to tell the others in the small group – without interruption – which words we chose, and to say why. When all who wish to do so have spoken, Robin invites a short exchange of responses and questions across the tables. Then there is a song, led by piano and flute, and the rector invites the Holy Spirit in an informal prayer.

Stage 4: Mission Action Planning

Robin briefly introduces the concept, illustrating it from a parish in the North-East.

Stage 5: Group reporting

(In the discussion of the questions before the away day, a sixth response had emerged that overlapped with questions 2 and 3.)

Robin invites each of the preparatory groups to make a presentation in turn: 1, 2, 3, 2/3, 4, 5, followed by clarifying questions or brief comments. *A member of the planning team warns when there are 2 minutes left in each reporting period.*

Report 1
Report 2
A brief break
Report 3
Report 4
Report 5
Report 6

A gentle reminder is given that everyone needs to take responsibility for listening to each group carefully.

Buffet lunch in the activity room, allowing for informal conversation.

Discerning leading themes

The shape of the afternoon session had been agreed, but the content could not be known until this point. During lunch the leadership team meets together to check on progress. What leading themes have emerged that might shape the work in the second half of the afternoon?

Process for the afternoon session

Stage 6: What are the emerging priorities?

The hosts reconvene their groups briefly, while members of the planning team offer their 'bids' for key themes to consider in the afternoon.

Robin and the planning team invite people to choose their theme and the leaders for that conversation direct people to a table or other space. Popular themes may need two groups. Some may not attract enough people. The themes of the conversation were worship, lifelong learning and spiritual development, pastoral care and communication.

Stage 7: Discerning the next steps for the church council to follow up

The theme groups are invited to summarize and share their insights, which are recorded on flip-chart sheets.

The rector leads a short time of prayer.

All return to their original tables to make recommendations of themes – with indicators – for the PCC to consider.

To reassure people that their work will make a difference:

- cards are provided inviting everyone to say where their interest lies and what they might offer – these to be read and responded to with a month by the planning team;
- a date is to be announced when the planning team will reconvene;
- a commitment to effective communication is made.

Prayer: I dream of a church

Although it was not in the programme, there came a moment when it occurred to Robin, as companion, that the poem 'The Dream', written by a former Bishop of Nevada, Wesley Frensdorff, could be adapted to give everyone a voice in a prayer catching theme of the day. This poem is readily found online. Robin briefly explained and then invited silence while each person wrote down a one-sentence prayer, beginning 'I dream of a church that . . .' Quietly, in turn, people spoke their prayer to the whole room. One of the leadership team offered to use computer skills to format a tapestry of the dreams to be displayed in church.

Review

We allow a short time to ask each person to say:

- What has been the most important moment for them in this meeting?
- What is their hope for the next steps?
- How do they see themselves as contributing?

Closing prayer

- A song led by the musicians.
- Robin leads a mutual form of blessing.
- The rector concludes the day, thanking people for their time and energy, ending by saying the meeting is now closed so that people are free to go or to stay and talk a while longer.

Press release

We sang, we prayed, we talked, we listened, and we pondered. The flesh was made comfortable in the pleasant surroundings of Abbeyfield's Grove House, and the spirit was quickened and encouraged as a way forward for St Peter's church began to be discerned. This was the Parish Away Day last Saturday. Facilitated by Robin Greenwood we spent the morning reflecting on the work done by the after-church groups and the Mums' Group a few weeks ago. Out of this emerged four themes which we looked at in groups after lunch. These themes – worship, lifelong learning (Continuing Spiritual Development was the phrase used by those familiar with Continuing Personal Development in their professional lives), pastoral care, and communication – and all the prayer and thinking that has gone on under these cryptic labels, will form the basis of our Mission Action Planning in the coming months.

(Published in the *Ilkley Gazette*, 19 March 2015, by Arthur Francis)

Planning to continue the conversation

The notes below were presented to the PCC (after acceptance by both the parish officers – the 'Standing Committee' – and the Annual Parish Church Meeting held just before the meeting of the newly elected council):

1 The following themes, which subsequently emerged from the morning session, were discussed at length and effectively will form the basis of Mission Action Planning, and in consequence will be placed as regular items on the PCC agenda.

2 It is envisaged that each theme will be managed and tasked by sub-groups, made up from interested members of the congregation. We hope that at least one or more members of the PCC will also participate in a particular sub-group so that each sub-group will be not only directly supported and encouraged by the PCC but will also have the opportunity to report regularly to the whole PCC.

3 Many of those who attended the Parish Away Day have already indicated their particular areas of interest or skills, and we intend to follow these up and invite them to take part if they wish. If you weren't able to attend the Parish Away Day but would like to contribute to one – or more – of the sub-groups, then please get in touch with those named below who have offered to co-ordinate the formation of the sub-groups.

4 We also recognized that there is an inevitable overlap between the four themes and one action within a theme can just as easily fit into another theme. We look forward to the sharing and cross-fertilization of ideas and suggestions between the sub-groups.

5 As you can imagine, in order to try and capture the very lively and engaging conversations revolving around the four themes during the afternoon would have taken an army of minute takers. Instead we have tried to summarize these as brief statements/action points, which we hope will act as hooks for each sub-group on which to hang more detail and specific actions. We also accept that plans will fall into short-, medium- and long-term timescales, so this will be an ongoing process.

6 Nevertheless you will notice that one particular action point has been highlighted within each theme, and we felt that these action points were either largely already in place, or more easily achievable, and recommend that each sub-group be tasked initially with these.

The four themes

1 Worship and spirituality

- Needs to be relevant and accessible
- Services

- To have a more informal service of worship at 4 p.m.
- Investigate alternative forms of worship, e.g. Taizé, Iona.
- Consider after-school discussion group.

- Buildings

  - To make the building an accessible and welcoming place.

2 Pastoral

- Devising and setting up of a visiting scheme to incorporate:

  - New members/welcoming
  - Lonely
  - Bereavement/loss
  - Illness
  - Weddings and baptisms
  - Spiritual

- Creating of database for those in pastoral need.
- Investigating and running courses for equipping/training visitors.

3 Learning and development

- Range of groups/courses:

  - Lent groups and house groups
  - Enquirers/access to Christian faith groups
  - Pilgrim course
  - Footsteps-style groups

- To create a learning atmosphere (for all levels).
- Identify training needs for group leaders and how best to meet them.
- Create action learning/activity groups.

4 Communication

- Talk/listen/feedback – reinforce value of basic communication among members.
- Create internal database – phone, email – with preference on how to be contacted.

- Research technology to aid worship, i.e. PA and audio visual systems.
- Collect attendance data, particularly at large services – Easter, Christmas, Remembrance.
- Build on existing networks, e.g. village and diocese websites.
- Research increased use of social media (e.g. Facebook), webcasting, live streaming.
- Consult CofE research and research best practice locally (all themes).

The expectation is that the PCC will invite leaders to recruit members to groups to prioritize and take these ideas forward. In several months' time a second away day, open to all, will receive reports and discern the way forward and discover what resources will be needed. The main themes will begin to structure each PCC meeting to avoid the disabling situation of a 'business as usual' and a 'Mission Action Planning' agenda competing with one another for resources of time, energy, people and money.

13   Becoming a more open church: a half-day conversation

> Wisdom formation most often requires guidance and support . . . openness to it and readiness to embrace it. And our churches have an important responsibility in helping this process to unfold.
>
> (Wimberly and Parker 2012, p. 17)

A gathering of representatives of the United Benefice of Barnoldswick with Bracewell, West Yorkshire.

Practical arrangements

- Twenty people participated, in a church hall several miles from the three churches involved.
- Through unforeseen circumstances, there had been no opportunity for Robin, as companion, to discuss the shape of the event with Diane Weaver, the vicar, or the church council.
- Chairs were arranged in a horseshoe, with a log-burning stove as a focus.
- A large oblong coffee table stood in the middle of the space.
- On the table were enough seed pods for all to have one each, and a large candle.
- Everyone was invited to bring food to share.
- Large font copies of the reading and of Psalm 147 had been prepared.

The process

Arrivals, refreshments and introductions

As companion, Robin invited everyone to listen as each person in turn spoke their name and explained their hopes for the event; these were written on sticky notes and placed on the table.

Listening to another church's story

A church leader from the local church told the story of how their congregation was seeking to be more open to the neighbourhood through social and ecological projects, involving young people and creating a welcome space for visitors.

Prayer

As companion, Robin led a prayer that all might be as open as possible to one another and to the Holy Spirit.

Dynamic Bible study: a paralysed man is healed (Mark 2.1–5, 11–12)

Following the *lectio divina* way of Bible reading, after a time of silence, people were invited to choose a word or phrase that resonated with them and to share it with one other person.

The companion then led an open conversation using the following prompts:

- What impact had the story of those who took a great deal of trouble to get a friend who was paralysed to Jesus?
- Do you have a fear of crowds, or of being closed in or stuck in a crowded room, a traffic jam, a full train?
- The paralysed man is trapped, but not by crowds.
- It is his body that stops him from moving.
- His useless legs close him off from others.
- They keep him from going out to meet this new prophet who has come to Capernaum.
- His friends open up a way for him to encounter Jesus.
- Imagine the scene – as they carry their friend to Jesus.
- Who thought of it?
- Who had the bold idea to break open the roof?
- What quality of love are they showing?
- Would we have done it?
- Or might we have said, 'Let's go tomorrow when the crowds might be less'?

They blessed their friend by enabling him to receive Jesus' blessing.

Do we find blessing through blessing others?

- They were not easily put off getting their friend to Jesus.
- Imagine how they felt when after all that work, they saw their friend walking.
- Who did this for you? When was that? What happened?
- Who, over the course of your life, has brought you to Jesus?
- Who can you do this for now?
- Do you know you're blessed to become a blessing?

We then gave thanks and wrote down the names of those who had brought us to Jesus, and listed opportunities now for us to do this for others. These were placed on the table.

Just before 11 a.m., several voices read the psalm of praise, Psalm 147.1–11.

Break for refreshments.

As companion, I asked if anyone had anything more to say from earlier in the morning.

Focusing on the wood-burning stove, we turned our attention to the next exercise.

Encountering God: the example of Moses (Exodus 3)

- God reveals his name as I AM (or 'I am here for you'), which both awes and encourages Moses to liberate his people from slavery.
- Jesus links himself with this name when he walks towards the frightened disciples on Lake Galilee: 'Take heart, it is I' (Matt. 14.27). Peter dares to walk on water while he keeps his eyes on Jesus.
- So a wood-burning stove is a symbol for daring to let God come close to awe and encourage us to go beyond what we believe is possible. What does this say about a 'welcoming church'? Responses to this included:

- warm
- focus for gathering
- also hot – reminder that we need a hot relationship with God in worship and prayer
- care
- creates space for many
- let the coldest sit nearest the fire.

The group then explored the slogan: **'Stop coming to church and become church'**.

In a welcoming church, all are guests of Christ but can also become hosts with Christ. As good hosts inviting people, what will be needed? To invite people there has to be:

- a genuine desire;
- careful preparation for different people and ages;
- willingness to be present to one another;
- a growing desire to be present to God;
- availability to all whom God loves in the world – leaving no one out.

To be hosts to others we must begin by welcoming Jesus ourselves. On the first Easter Day two dejected disciples walked without recognizing Jesus, but when they invited him into their home and he broke the bread and gave thanks – they recognized him and were filled with such joy that they immediately that night went all the way back to Jerusalem to tell others, and found they had had a similar experience (Luke 24.13–35).

This links with a recognition of Jesus as the centre of hope for ourselves and the world:

- Do we get it that we are blessed, welcomed – despite all we can say against ourselves?
- Do we recognize how hard it can be for others to come in?
- How would it be for you to go for the first time into a betting shop or mosque?
- To increase the range of people who can be part of your church community, how far could you stretch into a variety of kinds of music, prayer, learning and ways of talking together?

- List the ways you are already a blessing to your neighbourhood – recognizing thankfully that many others too are working here for the reign of God to come.

A check on practice: How hospitable are we?

We would claim to be a friendly, hospitable, welcoming church. Is that how we are seen and experienced?

Jesus' healing of the paralysed man reminded us that our salvation is not separate from that of our friends and neighbours. Dietrich Bonhoeffer chose to return from safety in the USA to be with his people as a pastor during the Nazi regime in Germany. He was sure that Jesus would ask him at his coming to heaven, 'Where are the others?'

We spent time in small groups asking the churches represented there to be more open to others:

- What do we have that we're proud of and want more of?
- What don't we have that we need?
- What do we have that we could do without?

The group wrote on a flip chart the things they wanted the church council to consider for their Mission Action Planning.

There were also ideas for a poster, a magazine article and a presentation to the three congregations on a Sunday.

As companion, Robin invited each person to pick up from the table a seed pod and to plant the seeds as a commitment to future growth.

A simple Eucharist

Around the coffee table there was a simple celebration of the Eucharist. People communicated one another and the final blessing was a mutual act, everyone giving and receiving the mark of the cross, saying 'May the Lord bless you deeply' and responding 'Amen'.

A shared lunch – this concluded the event.

Outcomes

Diane, the vicar, reflecting on that morning of conversation, wrote:

> I realize how much we covered that day and in such a short space of time. As for the outcomes – there is still so much to do! In direct response to the feedback received:

- The heating in Ghyll church has been improved.
- We are researching what families and young people want from church.
- The installation of a sound system is in the planning stage.
- The old coach house is now offered to wedding couples for refreshments while photographs are being taken.
- Plans are being formed to refurbish the kitchen area.
- As service to the community we have run Lent lunches once a week this spring. This has been a great success in terms of fellowship and raising money for the foodbank. It has also opened up our sense of how to be Church and made us more visible in the town.
- We held a quiz night in the church building, which also opened us to the community.
- Work has started to make the old vestry clean and useful.
- At the Annual Parish Church Meeting we shall continue by asking: 'What next?'

After a subsequent conversation with Robin as companion, Diane developed a conversational approach to the Annual Meeting. In her own words:

Barnoldswick and Bracewell Annual Parochial Church Meetings

What I did

My experience of APCMs was one of getting through the formalities as quickly as possible and then setting out the plans for the next 12 months while people listened. Having done one APCM using that model I wanted to do something differently. Meeting with Robin was the catalyst. I was able to lay out my disjointed thoughts and aims and with his support and suddenly it began to take shape, which meant I could make more coherent plans as to how the meetings would go.

I opened the APCM by explaining to people how we would be doing things slightly differently. A member of the PCC did a Bible reading on the Feeding of the Five Thousand (Matt. 14.13–21), which everyone had sight of. I then asked people to speak with their neighbour about what had come out of the passage for them. We then shared in a larger group and made a note of people's feedback on the flip chart. I reassured people at the outset that there were no wrong or right answers. Because of the group work my priest colleague, Claire Greenwood, had been doing during the previous 18 months, people shared willingly. I then went into my presentation. Unfortunately, due to the size and layout of the room I was unable to use the overhead projector but I gave people handouts so they could follow it. In my presentation I picked up the theme of 'abundance' from the Bible reading, reflected on all that had happened since myself and Claire had arrived in the parish and outlined what I believed were the four priorities, namely liturgy, children and families, opening up (ourselves and our churches) and admin (the need for admin support). I then asked people to share with their neighbour what they believed the priorities were before sharing in the larger group and making a note of the feedback on the flip chart. The plan is to take all these suggestions and discuss them at the next PCC, in the hope that people will be willing to work in small groups to take forward at least three priorities.

At this point we had a short comfort break and then moved into the formal business of electing people etc.

How people responded

As I am parish priest in two parishes, I held two APCMs using this model – the response was positive on both counts. The priorities for each parish were slightly different as were the outcomes. People were willing to engage and voice their opinions with confidence, which was very different from the experience of 12 months ago. I think this was because people were provided with the opportunity to speak, have grown in confidence through group work, and through experience have discovered that their opinions are both valued and acted upon. One email I received said: 'I particularly found this (APCM) interesting and an engrossing way of getting the attendees' attention and participation.'

What came out of it

At the end of the process there was a real buzz in the atmosphere – lots of conversations continued after the meeting. I did observe though, in myself and others, that part way through the process, as we were looking at what we wanted to do and acknowledging the limited resources (financially and people-wise), the energy dipped; but we seemed to work through that and end with a positive and hopeful expectation of what the future might hold. I am sure that beginning and ending the meetings being reminded of God's bounty and abundance had a positive impact.

(Vicar of Barnoldswick with Bracewell serving three churches (one town centre, two rural) in a population of 12,000+)

14 Conversations on poetry

Hospitality belongs not to the domain of exchange but to the domain of gift-giving. We ought not to expect as much (or more) out of hospitality as we put in. Every time exchange threatens to subvert what ought to be a gift, we should offer resistance.

(Volf 2010, p. 177)

Love: George Herbert

This example of a conversation outline on a poem might stand on its own or be part of another event. It could lead into preparing other meditations on poems and psalms.

Another further development could be to explore some of the psalms where 'blessing' – and related words such as 'happy', 'give thanks', 'glory', 'joy', 'praise' – provide a deep rhythm, for example, Psalms 1, 5, 7, 8, 9, 16, 18, 19, 24.

I am grateful to Malcolm Guite for pointing out how the seventeenth-century poet George Herbert's 'Love (III)' offers a beautiful and truthful route into exploring God's hospitality and blessing. Avoiding the word God, Herbert gives us a conversation between 'Love' and our soul, reluctant to believe we are blessed and welcome.

> LOVE bade me welcome; yet my soul drew back,
>   Guilty of dust and sin.
> But quick-eyed Love, observing me grow slack
>   From my first entrance in,
> Drew nearer to me, sweetly questioning
>   If I lack'd anything.
>
> 'A guest,' I answer'd, 'worthy to be here:'
>   Love said, 'You shall be he.'
> 'I, the unkind, ungrateful? Ah, my dear,
>   I cannot look on Thee.'
> Love took my hand and smiling did reply,
>   'Who made the eyes but I?'

> 'Truth, Lord; but I have marr'd them: let my shame
>   Go where it doth deserve.'
> 'And know you not,' says Love, 'Who bore the blame?'
>   'My dear, then I will serve.'
> 'You must sit down,' says Love, 'and taste my meat.'
>   So I did sit and eat.

In his assessment of Herbert's work and life, John Drury's comments on 'Love (III)' (Drury 2013, pp. 1–4) offer a framework for a conversation on blessing:

* Herbert wonders who it is he's up against all the time in his life; he prefers to answer 'Love' rather than 'God'. Maybe he felt it was just too complicated to say 'God' in the world in which he was living. How do you respond to that?
* Herbert avoids the arguments of religion to reach his last line, when the speaker surrenders, 'So I did sit and eat'.
* Read Herbert's poem aloud several times and keep some silence.
* Notice the subtle biblical references behind phrases such as 'guilty of dust and sin' (Adam, the primal man who sinned against his Creator); 'Who made the eyes but I?' (God the creator); '"know you not," says, Love, "who bore the blame?"' (Christ who took upon himself human sin and punishment) and the prophetic promise of a banquet for all creation finally redeemed.
* Look for references to Psalm 23.5, the Song of Songs 2.4 and Luke 12.37.
* Herbert asks a similar question to today about our sharing in the Eucharist. In his day some felt it appropriate to kneel and others to sit; we sit for a feast but kneel in our state of unworthiness. Today, kneeling (in penitence) and standing (as forgiven missioners) attract different viewpoints. What is this all about?
* What other connections do you make with these verses?

In a concluding prayer time, ask how this poem affects you: personally; as a group; as a church.

* How far are you still resisting love's way in preference to your own?
* How far are you now ready to live with ambiguity, subtlety and contradictions in yourself and church?

- In what ways is your capacity growing for: inclusiveness; difference; a sense of living in blessing?
- How could you allow yourselves to be like ripe apples ready to fall into God's hand?
- What prayer now forms?

15 Blessed to bless: young people as Church

Good conversation involves reciprocity and a balance between speaking and listening. It requires caring enough about the other to offer appropriate challenge on occasion, holding the other accountable, not simply glossing over faults and shortcomings.

(Linman 2010, p. 24)

St Wilfrid's, Newbiggin Hall.

Purpose of the conversation

The purpose of the conversation in an outer city 1960s housing estate in Newcastle was to explore how to make space for all ages to encounter God and one another, together. Twenty adult members of the congregation were present.

These are my briefing notes as companion, though as always with such events, following the conversation off the script and then back to it later has the potential to make the day more productive.

A local school head, Caroline, a committed worshipper at another church, had agreed to resource the event.

Sharing food (grace said by a church warden)

Bless, O Lord,
this food we are about to share,
and we pray you, O God,
that it may be good for both our bodies and souls.
Bless our meeting, conversation and decisions.
Especially we pray that we may learn to share
more deeply in this place between your friends
of every generation.
We pray in Jesus' name. **Amen.**

Moses' shining face (Exod. 34.29–35)

Each person had a large-font copy of the reading.
Several voices were invited to read beforehand.

- We noted the explosive moment when the holiness of God touches down and changes everything – this is not just a religious or spiritual experience but a time of threat and risk when our ordered world is shattered and nothing is the same again. We linked this to the resurrection events that changed the world for ever.
- Moses knew he was carrying the law but he didn't realize his face was shining from talking with God.

Jesus transfigured (Luke 9.28–36)

Again everyone had copies, and several voices spoke.

- The mountain is not named; perhaps it was Sinai.
- Peter, James and John were taken by surprise. They watched. While Jesus prayed, drawing near to talk with God, his face was changed. Familiar? Jesus talked with God, as Moses had done. And his whole body took on dazzling light, just like Moses'. What had happened to Moses was happening to Jesus.
- All the Jewish memory of God's holiness was caught up in the body of Jesus. He became the place where the holiness, the real oddity of God's presence was known, seen and available to all.
- The body of Jesus became the touching place where God was known to all people. They were terrified! They did not see Jesus as dumbed down, user-friendly, but the mixture of utter love and utter demand of God the Holy One.

Now we look at a third text.

Community created in blessing (2 Cor. 3.12—4.2)

God's holiness is what makes Christian community – church.

- Christians are not just ordinary people: we are made from God coming near, touching our personal and communal lives – if this is not true for all, then Christianity is nothing. There's no halfway point.

- We are called to be a blessing – and that is only possible if we are restless and hope-filled and alive in the whole of living, for the world, for the kingdom to come!
- For this to be real we need to stay connected to Jesus, seeing and showing the glory of God.
- Churches keep faith only by constantly remembering the life, death and resurrection of Jesus, endlessly telling the stories where Jesus showed the glory of God the Father, in everyday matters: a son comes home and is welcomed; a prostitute is forgiven and shown love; a leper is touched and cleansed; a woman who has been ill for years stands up and laughs and dances – a eucharistic pattern.
- The Church at Corinth is not called to be pious and separate but to let the memory of Jesus be so dazzling that it spills out into the world at large: God's holiness for the healing of many.

An integrated community

The conversation continued, asking how St Wilfrid's could integrate all ages as a matter of course. A warden welcomed Caroline, the local head teacher, and thanked her for giving time to help us be practical about monthly all-age worship. First though, the vicar, Sarah, invited those present at a previous conversation of hope to remind everyone of the issues about being open to all ages, all the time in various ways. Sarah summarized the points made (as listed below), inviting others to comment.

Exploring all-age worship

- Noise should be expected sometimes.
- Children can be involved in lots of appropriate ways.
- We can celebrate birthdays.
- Older people can take trouble to know the names of young ones.
- A variety of music should be offered so that all can join in (note what the children sing at school).
- Experiment with short hymns; use instruments.
- Intercessions can involve young ones if they are short, clear, slow and rehearsed, preferably with a microphone.
- Sermons can sometimes be interactive and visual.

- The Sunday school can display artwork in church – e.g. handprints.
- Young ones can take on practical jobs in church, e.g. ringing the bell, serving and welcoming, while adults happily take a back seat but with a watchful eye.
- Admission of children to communion should be explored.
- There need to be day trips to allow people of all ages to spend time together, getting to know one another.
- There will be implications for safeguarding – more CRB checks needed.

As companion, I reminded everyone of the honesty that had been expressed:

- Involving children – fears: potential for chaos, very time-consuming. At first, issues of security and safeguarding, making rules and boundaries, tension through age differences and different needs.
- Planning for monthly all-age worship: the visiting head teacher and the vicar pick up this conversation around issues raised, with comments from the facilitator.

The aim of this conversation – and the group work that may follow – is to increase commitment of those present so that a critical mass of church people may gradually take this forward.

A conclusion must include responses to the questions: Why, What, When and by Whom?

Widening the conversation

As companion, I had mapped out a possible shape for the conversation, as follows:

- Should we plan for an audit of what the children 'want' – ask them, find out where and what will engage them?
- How about holding an open meeting with parents/guardians?
- Could the church council include this in its Mission Action Planning – perhaps by developing a pattern of baptism visitors, keeping contacts updated, through an email bulletin, Facebook or blog? Who would lead and support this?
- Find out more about what the local schools do about faith teaching and experiences.

- Are there chances to lead assemblies in local schools?
- The types of service they have in schools, and their hymns and songs, could inform what church worship might offer.
- Suppose older members of the congregation became key to the imagining and planning of what emerges?
- Immediately encourage younger ones in church on Sunday to help in practical ways – giving and collecting books, helping to take the collection and ringing the bell. This will mean adults deciding to stand back supportively. How can we incorporate these ideas into the regular services?
- This is simply responding to a need and inviting the older members of the congregation to take their place in fostering the faith of the younger ones.

As a result, that church congregation became more responsible for love and for the actions and faith development of its young ones in practical and imaginative ways.

Sarah, the vicar of St Wilfrid's, wrote this postscript:

Postscript

We held our first all-age service on Easter Day 2015, a year after the conversation described. A crisis unfolded within the church in May 2014 when it was discovered that a large sum of money had been stolen. The church was left very short of funds and survived due to the help of Newcastle Diocese. A police investigation ensued, and this was concluded ten months later in March 2015. Holy Week and Easter following soon after were healing for the congregation of St Wilfrid's: the painful reality of what had happened was faced in the story of betrayal and crucifixion; there was grieving; then hope and the promise of a new future on Easter Day in our first all-age Eucharist.

We had invited the children in the congregation to come into church with their parents on Easter Eve to help make the Easter garden. The story of Holy Week and Easter was told as they did this. Then we had a conversation about the all-age Easter Day Eucharist, explaining that the children would lead the worship in new ways. Two children volunteered to work with the sidesmen to welcome the congregation and give out books, another two to collect books and tidy away at the end. A family agreed to bring up the offertory. A young reader rehearsed the short New Testament reading and two practised leading the intercessions together. At the service, the whole congregation was invited to make a recommitment of faith gathered around the font and to dip a finger in the water and make the sign of the cross on their forehead; the Easter Gospel was read in an interactive version by Rachel, a priest friend of the church, and all the congregation enjoyed joining in with actions and responses. A Sunday school leader led a talk on the gift of Easter with help from the children to unpack visual aids. A child helped to toll the church bell before the service and during the eucharistic prayer – which was interactive. Just before the blessing the children came forward to a special Easter tree placed by the altar, to collect gifts of small bags of chocolate eggs hanging from the branches and then to hang on the branches crosses with their names written on them and the words, 'Jesus died and rose again because he loves ME!' After the service the adults received chocolate eggs while the children enjoyed an energetic Easter-egg hunt – organized by a parent – in the garden outside.

This Easter Day Eucharist was truly joyful. Any fears on the part of the adults about all-age worship were allayed; it was informal without being chaotic; the children took part with commitment and enthusiasm and showed an ability to lead and read confidently and competently. Preparing, leading and participating in the worship drew the whole church family together.

The service signalled a new hope for St Wilfrid's after the darkness of the trauma the church had experienced.

16 A local shared-ministry team weekend

> We can come to God,
> Dressed for dancing
> Or
> Be carried on a stretcher
> To God's ward.
> > (Attributed to the Persian poet Hafiz)

Conference at Scargill House, Kettlewell, North Yorkshire, with a ministry team from All Saints, Hurworth, Darlington.

Purpose

- To find out more accurately our present position as the Shared Ministry Development Team.
- To know ourselves more deeply God's blessing to help us grow in our capacity to be a blessing to others.
- To draft key elements of a Mission Action Planning process for the parish – from the questionnaire and conversations this weekend.
- To discern a way to negotiate with the PCC and to take forward the process of Mission Action Planning, as a permanent feature of parish life.

Process

On the first evening there was supper and worship, before people 'checked in' with one another at the end of a working week, explaining 'What's going on in my life today, what I've temporarily left behind'. There was conversation on the aims of the weekend, prayer and relaxation.

The full day, Saturday, was entitled: 'Living in God's Blessing: Becoming a Church That is a Blessing'.

After breakfast on the Sunday there was a celebration of the Eucharist with the Community hosting the weekend. This ended with a final check up on future practicalities, some personal free time, lunch and departure.

Welcome, introduction and prayer

Two months beforehand, as companion, Robin had met with Adele Martin, the vicar, and two other members of the team to plan the day. The following is a detailed account of the planned shape of the process and content that emerged.

Prayer was led by Robin as companion, based on a careful reading of Psalm 19 and conversational reflection: 'Let the words of my mouth and the meditation of my heart be acceptable to you, O LORD, my rock and my redeemer' (v. 14).

The scriptural notion of blessing

As companion, Robin introduced blessing as a leading Christian theme. He worked from the notes below, inviting dialogue, comment and questions.

1 **Blessing in Scripture**

   (a) Every moment of the day is a blessed time when God can appear.

   (b) Throughout the Old Testament God's blessing is asked on every detail of living – blessing marks out the shape of living.

   (c) Scripture invites us to expect God in all things, people, relationships, conversations and actions.

   (d) Blessing is a potent and full experience of God who is both powerful and respectful – as we see in the words and actions of Jesus.

   (e) Blessing is always on the move – it is the biblical word for the constant interaction between God and the household or living system of creation.

2 **To be blessed is to be 'spoken well of'**

   (a) A person, animal, plant, situation or thing is 'spoken well of' (see Gen. 1.21–22). We are reminded of the primary goodness and potential given to every part of creation by God, in the way most appropriate to its nature and future.

(b) There is a *dynamic movement* between creation and God, in which there is no domination or manipulation.

3 Blessing as discernment

(a) Blessing is a combination of listening to and seeing what is real now.

(b) Blessing actively enables new possibilities.

4 Blessing is gift

(a) In blessing there is a deep logic of more, of overflowing abundance, 'my cup runneth over', of water into wine, of five loaves and two fish into twelve baskets of fragments.

(b) Blessing is a mutual and free 'to and fro' of love between God, the Trinity and the universe – it is the watermark in the paper of all creation.

(c) Blessing is like the alabaster jar of oil poured out over Jesus as a sign of his cross-shaped life and crucifixion, an unnecessary sign of God's providence; a gratuitous bestowal of something new, beyond reason or deserving.

(d) What examples in Scripture can we recall of this?

(e) As the word 'blessing' gets used a lot in everyday speech, we need to avoid superstition and sentimentality – partly by seeing it as relationship and not an act of power by an individual – and think about how its liturgical expression sometimes distorts its fullest meaning.

(f) We can rehabilitate blessing by exploring how the whole of God is active in the whole of the world.

5 Scriptural assumptions about blessing

(a) A leading theme in Scripture is that blessing is more than words spoken. It creates newness; it causes things to happen. So Moses, after the encounter of the burning bush, is enabled to step into his mission to save his people from slavery. Elizabeth, the mother of John the Baptizer, in blessing the pregnant Mary lifts her into becoming a blessing to others. Mary responds in the song we call 'Magnificat' – down the ages a practical inspiration to churches to seek out and serve the poor.

(b) In the Aramaic of Jesus' time the thrust of active beatitude seemed to be permission to be proactive for the poor and the prisoner.

(c) Blessing effects what is spoken, in line with God's word creating in Scripture. Blessing is an act of God or a person that makes a difference.

(d) We need to live in the blessing, make it actual for our lives.

(e) Our freedom to respond is the only thing in the world God does not have. See the prayer of surrender by Ignatius of Loyola:

> Take, O Lord, and receive my entire liberty, my memory, my understanding and my whole will. All that I am and all that I possess you have given me: I surrender it all to you, to be disposed of according to your will. Give me only your love and your grace; with these I will be rich enough, and will desire nothing more.

Refreshments were available as we continued.

Our own sense of being blessed

Conversation, *not discussion*:

* How blessed do we truly believe we are?
* How blessed is our church?
* Consider church as a 'wisdom community' – where knowledge and love, teaching and process meet, giving the community its character.

Lunch and time to reflect, with others or on our own.

Are there any insights from this morning?

God in particular places

* What's it like to live where your church is set?
* What goes well there? What not so well?

- How is the church as community and through us individually already an influence?
- We explored a previously completed congregational questionnaire – which responses do we notice especially?
- So what is now required and how could the churches be part of the answer?
- In partnership with which other groups?

Blessed for action

- So we have considered how we are blessed, we know we are called to become a blessing.
- Where does the specific role of your team come in?
- What role has the church council given to the team?
- How do the council, the team and the clergy work together?
- What needs to be re-addressed in this?
- How would you develop Mission Action Planning as a way of life, constantly reviewed and updated and the basis for every council meeting?
- A provisional list of actions for mapping was drawn up.
- What needs further conversation?
- What will be taken back to the church council, with recommendations?
- The elements of the Mission Action Plan (for now) to be written on a flip chart – a timescale for each item to be added.

Final prayer and supper.

After supper – getting practical.

- Who do we know who might lead on each item considered?
- It was decided that a whole PCC meeting be planned around this work.
- Fine-tuning the plan.

Prayer and rest

A time for people to be completely free to spend time alone or with the group as a demanding day closes.

Outcomes for Mission Action Planning

How does the Shared Ministry Development Team (SMDT) relate to the PCC?

PCC Responsible for strategy. SMDT develops priorities and recommendations in dialogue with PCC and community – some overlap of membership.

Finding out in what kind of place our church is set

- Commuter village – doubled in size since Second World War
- Population 3,000–4,000 (including next village – no church, one pub and reading rooms)
- A ribbon development
- Old weavers' cottages
- Medieval church building but Victorian rebuild
- Many older people
- Newcomers made welcome
- Good schools, dentist, physio and pharmacy
- Perceived as privileged place to live
- Village shop
- Five-star hotel attracting visitors
- Golf course/community centre/village hall
- Rockliffe Hall – Spa/Middlesbrough Training Ground
- Scouts and Brownies
- Churches – Church of England/Methodist/Christadelphians
- Safe place to grow up – youth club
- Community spirit – local fairs

How blessed is our church?

- Our vicar!
- The Reader
- Pastoral assistant in training

- Home communions
- Children's church
- Newsletter
- Prescription collection rota
- Baptism ministry
- Choir
- Congregational mix
- Wedding ministry
- Some much appreciated volunteers
- Music group
- Monthly prayer group
- Youth drop-in
- Lay funeral ministry
- Older people
- Summer and autumn fairs
- Flowers/coffee/bells/prayers/readers
- Christingle service
- Contribution of and to families

After the weekend, the church council had the opportunity to follow a similar process, using similar prompts for conversation. One of the realities to work with is that so many in the congregation have demanding work commitments and older ones share in the care and upbringing of younger members of their families.

To summarize, arising from the weekend the following priorities emerged for Mission Action Planning (see Table 2):

Table 2   Emerging mission action priorities

Welcome	Outreach
(Next six months) Lighting – new bulbs Refreshments – new machines and mugs Monthly welcome rota A board outside New banners by Christmas	Invitations – identify people to do this, e.g. Jill, Sue, Pat, Valerie, Judith Prescription rota Review impact of fairs etc. post-Easter Youth drop-in
Worship and spirituality	**Discipleship**
Review forms of worship for each Sunday 1st HC – alternate (position of table) 2nd 3rd 4th all-age worship 5th ecumenical Review monthly prayer meeting (1 year)	Preparation of introduction of 'The Story'
Finance	**Fabric**
Budget and cashflow required Increasing income – targets – updates Fundraising for major expenditure – GRANTS	Heating system Lighting of church centre and back of church Disabled and push-chair access Layout of church centre Relocate office and robing room Sound and projection system SEATING

17 Making a good ending

Blessing and conversation: a sermon

(Written jointly with Claire Greenwood.)

Preached in different forms in local churches to acknowledge and celebrate their part in the project.
Readings: Ezekiel 17.22–end; Mark 4.26–36

Today's first reading from Ezekiel began with a familiar but arresting phrase, 'Thus says the Lord GOD'; the passage from Mark's Gospel twice has the call to attend: 'Jesus also said'. It seems very like the phrase we use in worship, 'The Lord is here!' Not one to be taken lightly. The Bible's definition of a believer or disciple is one who *expects God's presence* and one who *listens when God speaks*. The early chapters of the book of Genesis make it clear that God's utterance makes things happen. God's speech gets everything into motion. God's words produce a result. And God seeks to be in partnership with those who will attend.

All through the Old Testament it is listening and responding that creates the tribes called 'Israel' as 'God's people'. Listening attentively to God creates a bond of belonging and following: a covenant. Listening expectantly is the doorway to a deepening relationship with God, with other people, with creation and with ourselves.

In the New Testament the listening is especially to Jesus – as he presents God's kingdom. In which normal expectations about everything – love, justice, reconciliation – are turned upside down. Jesus starts his earthly ministry with the cry 'repent' (in Greek, *metanoia*). We lessen its impact when we limit this to an appeal for sharper morality. *Metanoia* means 'turn around', 'take a second look', 'get a completely new way of seeing everything'.

Today's Gospel characterizes that kingdom as one of growth beyond any human expectation. Luxuriant plants grow from tiny seeds, with very little interference or assistance from us. God's kingdom grows and bears fruit simply because God has spoken. God at work in the world is a God who brings about impossibilities, or as Scripture says, 'wonders'.

The first time I was with you I was starting a research programme. The purpose was to help congregations grow in confidence. It was to find an antidote to the anxiety and pathos found in many churches today. We can remember golden days in the past when faith was readily accepted in society and when churches were held in high regard and there were enough clergy to keep the system working well. The two leading themes I worked with have been 'blessing' and 'conversation'. The book that has emerged from this, *Sharing God's Blessing*, is intended for churches to use at any time but especially when they are in the middle of change of some kind.

I'm grateful that some of you have taken time to road-test the fruits of my work in your Lent course this year. I have found your feedback helpful in the final editing for publication.

So the first theme was that God blesses us and invites us to be a blessing to others. The scriptural notion of blessing is about knowing we are spoken well of, by God, so as to thrive. Second, I took the concept of conversation – which goes a long way beyond discussion. 'Discussion' is debate; it is combative – it's about cutting your opponent to pieces. *Discutio* is its Latin root – to show your position as the most correct. 'Conversation' is about being really *present*, listening carefully to one another so that there can be an opening for the transformation of people and of Church and society. One of Jesus' core messages is that we can all respond to God's saying to us, 'You are my beloved'. He enacted this at his baptism in the Jordan and continued inviting people to hear this word from God to them and to respond. When we choose to hear God's call, anything is possible. Scripture is not just historical narrative or God's word dictated direct from heaven. It's a vehicle, involving many human experiences of listening to God and responding, and not hearing and not responding – a vehicle that holds the possibility of bringing God's word to us, as church and as people, here and now, today, inviting us to listen and respond. Whatever the Holy Spirit was saying to us yesterday was well and good; but he moves us on, enquiring, 'So what is God calling out from us today and tomorrow?' When Scripture is read – no less than when bread and wine are blessed – God, the speaker, is *present*, inviting us also to be present and to see the world as God sees it. Whether we're reading Scripture alone or with others, we are invited to make room for the indwelling of God and for the indwelling of the whole of creation and its people: to pay attention to and trust what we're hearing. Scripture invites us to become what we hear. That means listening with the whole of ourselves and not just our brain. It's what Scripture means by listening with 'the heart';

inviting God to re-forge our deepest selves into what we can become. Scripture recreates us personally and us as Church when we go beyond seeing Scripture as just lessons read in the service or the Bible read at home – to welcoming Godself into our deepest centre, to make us signs of what Jesus calls 'the kingdom' or 'reign' of God.

I hope that churches that have taken part in some of the conversations on blessing will have discovered how to listen, really listen to one another, how to be respectfully *present* to one another, without trying to prove the other wrong. And I hope that the book for leaders that has emerged from the two-year project will play a part in training ourselves and many others to remember Jesus' basic message that we live within God's love: that God cares about us, runs to meet us when we've wandered off, knows us better than we know ourselves, weeps with us, laughs with us, pushes and shoves us, inspires us, judges us, forgives us – wraps us up protectively, encourages us to be independent, awes us into stillness or releases shouts of laughter – Jesus was crucified because religious people couldn't accept his way of showing who God is.

When I spoke about all this at a conference a few months ago, I was surprised and disappointed that the very first person to ask a question stood up and said accusingly 'And what about original sin?'

I didn't have a ready answer but I thought about it later. Of course we have to acknowledge the mess the world is in, of which we are a part. But Scripture insists that it's not either/or – the truth we're slow to learn is that God loves us whether we're 'good' or whether we're 'bad'. We're God's beloved whether we know it or not, and are invited to grow into that identity as fully as we can. But accepting that we are loved is not always easy. It involves taking the place of daughters and sons with God as our father. The moment we truly believe we are blessed by God's love is the moment when things get tricky – being loved changes a person; old certainties shift and melt; new feelings come to the surface, which can be confusing; we see ourselves slightly differently and so we see others differently too.

Yes, it's hard work to keep remembering to love, and trusting that you *are* loved – and that there's enough to go around – because God is the source of all loving and made us in his own image. It's hard for families to hold themselves within God's blessing, and it's hard for church communities to do the same. The more we care and are passionate about our values and beliefs, the harder it is to dedicate ourselves to listening as well as speaking: being polite and courteous, and respectful to others, even if we think, frankly, that they're wrong. We don't have to be a doormat, and lose hold of our beliefs, but we can get interested in the to and fro, the shifts between certainty and uncertainty, that happen in a good conversation. Like mixing up a casserole – the sum is greater than its parts. Something new and lively is created – even if our individual clarity is temporarily destroyed. This is what the Scripture readings say to me, today. That God will plant us on a high and lofty mountain to produce fruit and to be shelter to those in need. Or to be the grain that erupts from a tiny seed. Blessing is an ecology – creation blesses God, God blesses creation, God blesses us, we bless God, other people bless us and we bless them and so on. Often we are recipients of blessings; sometimes we are the origin of blessings – Jesus is saying 'Yes, go on, be a blessing to the poor, those in need, the prisoner, and the hungry – by being a blessing you will know just how much you are blessed. However small your faith – like a tiny seed it can become something beyond your imagining and be of benefit to society and the wider world.' As I come to the end of this two-year research fellowship at Durham University, I would hope that the word 'blessing' will trigger something in you – maybe for the rest of your life – that connects with Jesus' teaching about the kingdom and about eternal life:

- That you will believe that you are deeply blessed by God – and remind yourself of this when you feel miserable, confused, despairing or generally unloved and unloving. Discipline is required for creating this kind of habit.
- That you will discover that this transforms you, as individuals and as a community, into *being* a blessing – a loving force, born of the Spirit, a child of God – whatever phrase makes sense to you.
- That you keep the conversations going as part of church life. It is when we risk talking together of God that we discover all our different stories and see each other in a new light. This is a never-ending process, because if we do it right – respectful to each other and hanging on to God's word in the Scriptures – other people will want to join in and we will be changed too. Our society is desperate to find out if conversations can go as deep as this without fights breaking out.

Just for a moment now –

> In quietness, know that you are blessed –
> by God, who is Father, Son and Holy Spirit.
> And now, know that you are a blessing to others –

through the creating of the Father,
the companionship of the Son
and the inspiration of the Spirit. **Amen**.

Final review day

(Brunswick Methodist Church, Newcastle, June 2015)

Brunswick Methodist Church in Newcastle city centre was a key point of hospitality throughout this two-year research process. To bring together representatives of participating churches in the North-East to say 'Thank you', to reflect on what had been learned and to bless one another for the next step seemed very appropriate. Brunswick's pervading spirit of daily welcome to all ages and nationalities is well expressed by deacon Eunice Attwood, a former staff member: 'I want to be part of a church that offers outrageous grace, reckless generosity, transforming love and engaging faith' (Ministerial Team Leaflet 2015).

Team meeting to arrange the space around small tables and be ready to welcome those attending: Robin, Rachel Wood and Malcolm Grundy.

Welcome, prayer, and shared food.

Introduction

A summary by Robin of the process and experiences of the past two years, the importance of going beyond words to identifying feelings and taking action. A reminder of the two leading themes of blessing and conversation. Responses from those attending gave everyone a chance to clarify what they had found significant. I had been concerned that not enough people would see the point in giving time to this ending. In the event the 20 who were present – some arriving late, some leaving early because of other commitments – created a strong atmosphere to bring closure to the project. This was another lesson in trusting others to share 'leadership' rather than trying to control or push the river as solo 'leader'.

A period of prayer, including *lectio divina* (Isa. 6.1–8), led by Rachel.

Malcolm drew people into groups of four from the different contexts to have conversations on:

- What part of the two-year project have I taken part in?
- What was it like for me?
- What difference might it have made to me and to my church?

Responses and questions presented to the whole meeting included:

- Noting who had been part of local meetings led by Robin, the road-testing of the five conversations in Lent 2015, giving feedback for improving the five structured conversations before publication and the two gatherings of the participating churches.
- Celebrating the ecumenical dimension that had brought very different experiences of Church together to listen to one another.
- The value of having a 'companion' to walk with conversation groups, especially in giving others confidence to 'speak out' and sometimes gently leading people to be more daring.
- Valuing a growing ability to hold conversations – for example, about 'What do we mean by *spiritual*?' – and a general perception that, through this process, congregations had grown in their willingness to speak more directly to one another about God's active *presence*.
- Anxiety was expressed by some that, as with all church talk, there was a danger of returning to the same ground and not moving beyond it.
- This led into discussion about what might be a clear vehicle for transformation, such as: a crisis through which more felt called to participate rather than 'leaving it to the few'; leaders with facilitation skills; an outside agency; identifying an objective and focusing on it and deciding who is responsible for taking it forward and making sure they have adequate support and feedback; regular review or a culture of continuing conversation. Some believed that coming to know that the community was 'living in blessing' or 'acting as a blessing' was a vehicle for transformation in itself.
- The question was raised whether having structured conversations limited the freedom for theology to arise from within a group.
- Many spoke of the value for churches of talking together regularly about their life with God, in confidential conversation including prayer and attending to Scripture, rather than just attending planning meetings. Growth in friendship, love and trust were

recognized as products of conversation where confidentiality was openly agreed.

- Some had been on a learning journey about knowing when to speak and when to listen.
- There was an exchange about how conversation had helped a greater number within a congregation to see the bigger picture.
- One church especially explored how engaging with the notion of being blessed to become a blessing had been a key to remaining a 'Christian' community through a period of severe trauma.
- Some spoke of the benefits of being encouraged both to recognize their feelings and to include them in conversation.
- All spoke of continuing conversation in various ways and the value of being challenged to move on from previous assumptions about 'how things are'.

Pause for refreshments.

Robin encouraged clergy present to respond by telling the story of the project from their perspective. They affirmed many of the points made above as well as reminding the meeting of regional and diocesan responses to some of the pressing issues for churches in this period of transition. Particular issues mentioned:

- The benefits of local leaders from different churches, ecumenically, committing to purposeful prayer and conversation on how the future can be very different if we dare to give up the struggles to keep old systems in place out of misplaced loyalty to the past or even to leaders who do not 'get it'.
- The tendency for churches regionally still to assume that all clergy, often acting alone, can function across a wide range of tasks. This led to a call for the creative management of human resources, linked with the hopes and fears of people locally and an imaginative and varied approach to how groups of churches could best be stimulated and led.
- It was noted that conversation for scaling across ideas and resources, through local networks, has more capacity to bring about changes in practice than the continuing habit of setting up a task group under the leadership of a 'significant person' to produce a report planning for structural innovation.

Groups of four again to have a further conversation (Malcolm and Rachel): 'What practical and emotional difference might come from this project for my church?'

Some of the responses:

- It has helped us cross denominational boundaries.
- We've started looking first at how we are blessed rather than always starting with problems.
- Blessing is more than words; we've discovered the power of blessing as an impetus to get us moving.
- At the heart of being Church is thankfulness – focused in eucharistic worship – a gift to be used and shared, which in turn leads to encouragement and action.
- These conversations lead to the empowerment of 'ordinary' people; it's good to see the liberation or freedom when it happens.
- This liberation will grow more when the 'hierarchy' trust it and relinquish their need to control from the centre.
- How will we continue to make sure more and more different voices can be heard?
- Blessing is not a sentimental matter. Scripture and experience remind us that blessing brings challenge and growth as well as resources. Many who were blessed by God in Scripture were given strength to travel very difficult paths to bring healing and reconciliation to others.
- Our church has learnt more about listening to one another, communicating, negotiating and being companions to others.
- We want our church has take on the practice of blessing, which means some dismantling of old ways of seeing things.
- Let's see ourselves as 'companion saboteurs' rather than allowing conversation to become the new 'must do' or 'orthodoxy' – which will kill it off for sure. Let's pledge to bring it in by stealth. Wherever we have influence, let's, quietly, just make sure that from now on, *this is our natural way of being Church.*

Malcolm led a brief final session: 'What could all this teach us and the wider Church to which we belong?'

Some principles emerged:

- To encourage the wider church to come out of its castles and to use participatory action and conversational ways to imagine, plan for and wrestle with change.
- To recognize that whether we know it or not God knows us as 'beloved'.
- To live consciously in blessing so that nothing is impossible.
- To start small and connect with others.
- To see Church by definition as open and capable of unlocking the lives of people, communities and places.

Celebration, thanks and final blessing and commissioning.

The gathering closed with Robin thanking the churches represented for their participation in creating the book that would emerge, and reminding everyone that they had given hours of their time and love to be a blessing to all who in the future might work in local churches with support from the book.

The gathering closed with an act of mutual blessing. With the words 'May the Lord bless you deeply', people moved around freely signing one another with the mark of the cross on their forehead.

Later on the same day Robin met with representatives of students and young adults with their leader Jill Foster, who had taken part in road-testing the five conversations. Features of their response included the benefits of conversation for building confidence in faith as well as in relationships and the significance for church communities of seeking transformative and inclusive forms of learning and reading Scripture, rather than automatically privileging the academic and analytic.

18   A journey just beginning

Perhaps most important, help people commit to living the principle of Appreciative Inquiry and positive change. In particular, use inquiry, storytelling, and narrative analysis to make decisions – and to consider, introduce, and recognize organizational changes. Tell and retell the stories behind systemic changes that have since become a way of life.

(Whitney and Trosten-Bloom 2003, p. 119)

Values and practices

If conversation-based change is a valuable holistic discipline for churches in transition, what further resources are required? Rather than attempting to match up reality to idealized 'models', I have found it more productive to introduce to churches the notion of enquiring into their core values and the habits that demonstrate them.

- How do you follow Jesus in this place?
- What are the values you would die for?
- How do they become a new culture and ethos that will continue to guide your Mission Action Planning?
- How would you test your performance?
- Are they just the aspirations of a few people or of one pioneering area of work? How can these values and habits be scaled across every dimension of a diocese or group of churches acting together?

A culture change

Although change is not the most attractive idea for many churches, currently church synods, leadership courses and websites demonstrate a sustained concentration on organizational change. As I have emphasized, I am convinced that for our approach to be at a deep enough level to make a difference, it has to be holistic and multidisciplinary. My years of working on church development, and especially the two years of this William Leech research project, encourage me to list the following moves to resource transformational change.

1 **To live from blessing**

Through worship, sacraments, Scripture, and practising Spirit-led community, we can learn to recognize the abundance of God as a gift. Whatever difficulties churches are facing, in terms of the attitude of society, problems of money and buildings or apparent lack of ministers, nothing seems the same when we allow ourselves to find or be found by God's blessing – through pursuing agendas of justice and mercy or sharing in praise, Scripture reading, Eucharist or contemplation. Unlearning habits of self-protection – dismantling – must be a gift we demand for ourselves from God.

2 **To know we have more than enough**

Jesus' feeding of the crowds or his sending out of disciples in training open us to the long scriptural tradition of believing we have what it takes to demonstrate God's own generosity. The practice of being neighbours, agents of healing, disturbers of complacency in the face of poverty and, like Jesus, being unprotected self-givers, is what creates Church. As Moses and the Israelites' desert journey reminds us, learning to live in blessing is not a linear process. From the attitude that we'll share faith and justice one day, when we have enough, we're called to recognize that for God's beloved, now is the moment to give.

3 **Travelling in conversational change**

As the disciples experienced on the Emmaus road or Philip and the Ethiopian official on the road to Joppa, conversation can reveal unexpected newness from God. Persuading cerebral Christians to experiment slowly with the emotions and respectful listening could be a miraculous source of the blessing churches need today. The detailed steps illustrated in this book will I hope inspire and encourage further experiment in multiple situations.

4 **Fostering companions**

Dioceses or mission areas might already recognize in a few people the charism of facilitation or companioning. To provide regular opportunities for local churches to flourish through this ministry requires first of all the recognition of the vital importance of this by those with influence. As with all ministries, there needs to be a balance between the needs of churches for wise and effective companioning and discernment of the attitude and skills of those offering to meet that need. In the book I have highlighted the need for companions to have the maturity to know how to fulfil the role in an assured but vulnerable and humble manner. Effective companions will need networks to sustain them as reflective practitioners.

The companion is one who helps the group: to listen to stories while recognizing that each is just one narrative among many; to persuade and show people how to listen deeply; to encourage positive questioning; and observe themselves in growing in mature relationship. Observing where the role of companion has been fruitful could be the way to knowing who to recruit and how to resource those called to a very distinctive role. The difficulties, however, should not inhibit regional leaders from taking practical steps to increase the number of available companions and arrange for their deployment and support.

5 **Leader formation**
Given our churches' history and the often high age profile of congregations, whoever is called to be pastor, leader, priest, Reader or bishop has a disproportionate influence on the values and practices of the local church. If that is a given, it is likely that the majority of people concerned with the dynamics of local churches will remain comfortable with various forms of hierarchy, debate and discussion, rather than with mutual patterns of working, holistic culture and listening to the voices of all. It must be of immense importance, therefore, that the recruitment, discernment and formation of women and men for church ministries now offers a deliberate counterbalance.

Churches urgently need in leadership those who have the gifts and maturity to lead and manage through conversational practice, and who are committed to increasing their competence in planning and in being trusting companions to adult Christian learning to form many in reflective practice. Training courses for clergy and Readers are notoriously overloaded with 'essential' elements that must somehow be crammed in, as though that were the end of all learning. Education for leaders needs to assume a growing participatory culture so that not all bishops need to be able to read spreadsheets and some clergy will foster their church's talents for creativity through poetry, drama and music. Colleges and courses could learn more from change-management theory/practice to trust more in teaching students how to prioritize the slow but determined fostering of values and habits in the whole church. Yes, society is in many respects degrading and churches themselves are at risk of losing their identity. But panic measures of conformity and control are not the answer. So we now require leaders not to tell others what they know or should know, nor to fix things that are broken, but to believe in processes and be effective in creating and generating conversation-based transformation. Do we have the courage to go with others to places where neither we nor they have ever been before?

Not by bread alone

> The bene . . . diction aims to situate us in the story of this God so that we are freed from all other masters and powers in our lives . . . [it] assures us that *a life of obedient discipleship* is the clue to well-being from this God who remains faithfully among those in covenant with him.
>
> (Brueggemann 2011, p. 281; emphasis in original)

This book will I hope open new doors into how churches engage with God's mission out of the burning energy of God's own initiative. It is God who, minute by minute, miraculously, against all odds, is creating Church as an embodiment of thanksgiving and praise. A truly eucharistic Church – in thousands of ways – knows it is blessed in order to become a blessing to others; although through this two-year period of research I have come to recognize how saying it that way is to put a straitjacket on God. Blessing as an ecology, moving fluidly has become clearer to me and I hope will be for many an inspiration for continuing conversations rooted in blessing.

Participative study of Scripture – *lectio divina* – has been a crucial element in the conversations in this book. It is an icon of a conversation-based invitation to transformation. It seems appropriate now to leave the future poised. Shall we follow God in God's way of blessing or shall we settle for less?

Lectio *for a ministry team, bishop's staff meeting or leadership group*

Read slowly Matthew 4.1–11:

> Then Jesus was led up by the Spirit into the wilderness to be tempted by the devil. He fasted for forty days and forty nights, and afterwards he was famished. The tempter came and said to him, 'If you are the Son of God, command these stones to become loaves of bread.' But he answered, 'It is written,
>
> "One does not live by bread alone,
> but by every word that comes from the mouth of God."'
>
> Then the devil took him to the holy city and placed him on the pinnacle of the temple, saying to him, 'If you are the Son of God, throw yourself down; for it is written,
>
> "He will command his angels concerning you",
> and "On their hands they will bear you up,
> so that you will not dash your foot against a stone."'
>
> Jesus said to him, 'Again it is written, "Do not put the Lord your God to the test."'
>
> Again, the devil took him to a very high mountain and showed him all the kingdoms of the world and their splendour; and he said to him, 'All these I will give you, if you will fall down and worship me.' Jesus said to him, 'Away with you, Satan! for it is written,
>
> "Worship the Lord your God,
> and serve only him."'
>
> Then the devil left him, and suddenly angels came and waited on him.

In silence consider, on your own, for a while: Which word or phrase stands out for you today?

In twos and then in the group, share your choice and reflect on it.

Some prompts for conversation:

* Matthew's Gospel presents Jesus' story as a resource for a new way of being human.
* Jesus' mission from the Father was to displace outworn rigid ways in favour of the rule of God.
* Church communities are places for practising and showing Jesus' way of yielding to God.

- Parallel with the experience of Jesus, in the desert and throughout his ministry, when churches attempt to live in obedience to the Father, they find themselves both testing out God's reliability and thinking of ways to work around the call to follow as disciples in total loyalty.
- When Jesus had remained obedient to the Father (and not chosen a smaller agenda), angels came to minister to him.

Keep a silence for at least five minutes and then let another person reread the text. Are there new things to be said about conversation, compromise, power, blessing and our particular responsibilities for keeping churches connected to God? Finally, reread the text through another voice.

Jesus shows us how, together and alone, we can come to stand in the same place as himself, before and in God. His healing and reconciling ministry shows us the blessing God has for us and desires to draw from us, for the world's healing. These words of Pope Francis, though directed towards us personally as Christians, can equally invite our churches to stop talking about God and make spaces for all to be called out of the present world's version of life to one that shares communion with the God of unspeakable abundance, who draws us with the whole creation to beatitude.

I see clearly that the thing the Church needs most today is the ability to heal wounds and to warm the hearts of the faithful; it needs nearness, proximity. I see the Church as a field hospital after battle. It is useless to ask a seriously injured person if he has high cholesterol and about the levels of his blood sugars! You have to heal his wounds. Then we can talk about everything else. Heal the wounds, heal the wounds ... And you have to start from the ground up!
(Interview with Pope Francis, in Estrada and Toldy 2014, p. 103)

References and further reading

Allatt, John and Campling, Penelope (2011/2013), *Intelligent Kindness: Reforming the Culture of Healthcare*, London: RCPsych Publications.

Amirtham, Samuel and Pobee, John S. (eds) (1986), *Theology by the People: Reflections on Doing Theology in Community*, Geneva: WCC.

Anderson, John and Bilfeldt, Annette (2012), 'The role of Action Research: The Case of Public Elder Care in DK, Planning Studies (Plan, By og Proces)', Paper for the 26th Conference of the Nordic Sociological Association 2012 – <https://notendur.hi.is/shj/.../Actionresearch.nordic.Soc. 2012>.

Basset, Lytta (2007), *Holy Anger: Jacob, Job, Jesus*, London: Continuum.

Bianchi, Enzo (2015), *Lectio Divina: From God's Word to our Lives*, London: SPCK.

Boff, Leonardo (1985), *Church, Charisma and Power*, London: SCM Press.

Browning, Don S. (1999), *A Fundamental Practical Theology: Descriptive and Strategic Proposals*, Minneapolis, MN: Fortress Press.

Brueggemann, Walter (1978), *The Prophetic Imagination*, Philadelphia, PA: Fortress Press.

Brueggemann, Walter (1984), *The Message of the Psalms*, Minneapolis, MN: Augsburg.

Brueggemann, Walter (1997), *Theology of the Old Testament, Testimony, Dispute, Advocacy*, Minneapolis, MN: Fortress Press.

Brueggemann, Walter (2002), *Ichabod Toward Home: The Journey of God's People*, Cambridge: Eerdmans.

Brueggemann, Walter (2003), *Awed to Heaven, Rooted in Earth: Prayers of Walter Brueggemann*, Minneapolis, MN: Fortress Press.

Brueggemann, Walter (2007), *Praying the Psalms: Engaging Scripture and the Life of the Spirit*, 2nd edn, Eugene, OR: Wipf & Stock.

Brueggemann, Walter (2011), *The Collected Sermons of Walter Brueggemann*, Louisville, KY: Westminster John Knox Press.

Brydon-Miller, Mary (2003), 'Why Action Research?', *Action Research* 1:1, 9–28.

Burrows, Ruth (1989), *Interior Castle Explored*, London: Sheed & Ward.

Capra, Fritjof and Steindl-Rast, David, with Matus, Thomas (1991), *Belonging to the Universe: Explorations on the Frontiers of Science and Spirituality*, New York: HarperSanFrancisco.

Chacour, Elias, with Jensen, Mary E. (2001), *We Belong to the Land: The Story of a Palestinian Israeli Who Lives for Peace and Reconciliation*, Notre Dame, IN: University of Notre Dame Press.

Church of England (2014), *The Beatitudes: A Course for the Christian Journey*, London: Church House Publishing.

Clark, Jonathan (2013), 'Inclusive Catholicity', in Gittoes et al. (eds) 2013.

Clinton, M. (2014), *Experiences of Ministry 2013 Report: Role Specific Development Programme*, London: King's College.

Conway, Stephen (2013), 'Generous Episcopacy', in Gittoes et al. (eds) 2013.

Drury, John (2013), *Music at Midnight: The Life and Poetry of George Herbert*, London: Penguin.

Duck, Ruth C. and Wilson-Kastner, Patricia (1999), *Praising God: The Trinity in Christian Worship*, Louisville, KY: Westminster John Knox Press.

Ernst, Sheila (1981/1985), *In Our Own Hands: A Book of Self-Help Therapy*, London: Women's Press.

Erskine, Noel Leo (2008), *Black Theology and Pedagogy*, New York: Palgrave Macmillan.

Estrada, Rui and Toldy, Teresa Martinho (2014), 'Pope Francis' Emphasis on Charity', *Concilium* 2014:4, pp. 101ff.

Ford, David F. (1999), *Self and Salvation: Being Transformed*, Cambridge: Cambridge University Press.

Ford, David F. (2007), *Christian Wisdom: Desiring God and Learning in Love*, Cambridge: Cambridge University Press.

Ford, David F. (2014), *The Drama of Living: Becoming Wise in the Spirit*, Norwich: Canterbury Press.

Ford, David F. and Hardy, Daniel W. (2005), *Living in Praise: Worshipping and Knowing God*, London: Darton, Longman & Todd.

Fox, Matthew (1983), *Original Blessing: A Primer in Creation Spirituality*, Santa Fe, NM: Bear & Company.

Freire, Paulo (1970, 1993), *Pedagogy of the Oppressed*, rev. edn, London: Penguin.

General Synod (2015), 'In Each Generation: A Programme for the Renewal and Reform of the Church of England', GS 1976 and GS 1124 (November 2015), London: Archbishops' Council <www.churchofengland.org>.

Gittoes, Julie, Green, Brutus and Heard, James (2013), *Generous Ecclesiology: Church, World and the Kingdom of God*, London: SCM Press.

Goens, Linda M. (1999), *Praising God Through the Lively Arts*, Nashville, TN: Abingdon Press.

Greenwood, Robin (1988), *Reclaiming the Church*, London: Collins.

Greenwood, Robin (2013), *Being Church: The Formation of Christian Community*, London: SPCK.

Grundy, Malcolm (2015), *Multi-Congregation Ministry: Theology and Practice in the Local Church*, Norwich: Canterbury Press.

Guite, Malcolm (2013), *The Singing Bowl: Collected Poems by Malcolm Guite*, Norwich: Canterbury Press.

Hahnenberg, Edward P. (2014), *Theology for Ministry: An Introduction for Lay Ministers*, Collegeville, MN: Liturgical Press.

Hardy, Daniel W. (2001), *Finding the Church*, London: SCM Press.

Hardy, D., with Hardy Ford, D., Ochs, P. and Ford, D. F. (2010), *Wording a Radiance: Parting Conversations on God and the Church*, London: SCM Press.

Harris Thompsett, Fredrica (2004), *We are Theologians: Strengthening the People of God*, New York: Seabury Press.

Harter, Michael (ed.) (2005), *Hearts on Fire: Praying with Jesuits*, Chicago: Loyola Press.

Hasson, Gill (2015), *Mindfulness Pocketbook: Little Exercises for a Calmer Life*, Chichester: Capstone.

Heard, James (2013), 'Inculturation – Faithful to the Past: Open to the Future', in Gittoes et al. (eds) 2013.

Heron, John (1999, 2010), *The Complete Facilitator's Handbook*, London: Kogan Page.

Hoffmann, Laurence A. (1990), 'Rabbinic Berakhah and Jewish Spirituality', *Concilium*, 1990:3, pp. 18–30.

Hollis, James (1998), *The Eden Project: In Search of the Magical Other*, Toronto: Inner City Books.

Hollis, James (2001), *Creating a Life: Finding Your Individual Path*, Toronto: Inner City Books.

Hollis, James (2013), *Hauntings: Dispelling the Ghosts Who Run Our Lives*, Asheville, NC: Chiron Publications.

Hunter, Alastair (2006), *Wisdom Literature*, London: SCM Press.

Janzen, David (2013), *The Intentional Christian Community*, Brewster, MA: Paraclete Press.

Jenkins, Timothy (1999), *Religion in English Everyday Life: An Ethnographic Approach*, New York and Oxford: Berghahn Books.

Jenkins, Timothy (2006), *An Experiment in Providence: Faith Engages with the World*, London: SPCK.

Kegan, Robert and Lahey, Lisa Laskow (2014), *Immunity to Change*, Boston: Harvard Business Press.

Keller, Catherine (2003), *Face of the Deep: A Theology of Becoming*, London and New York: Routledge.

Kujawa-Holbrook, Sheryl A. and Thompsett, Fredrica Harris (2010), *Born of Water, Born of Spirit*, Herndon, VA: Alban Institute.

Laloux, Frederic (2014), *Reinventing Organizations: A Guide to Creating Organizations Inspired by the Next Stage of Human Consciousness*, Brussels: Nelson Parker.

Lebacqz, Karen (1997), *Word, Worship, World and Wonder: Reflections on Christian Living*, Nashville, TN: Abingdon Press.

Lewis, Sarah, Passmore, Jonathan and Cantore, Stefan (2008), *Appreciative Inquiry for Change Management: Using AI to Facilitate Organizational Development*, London: Kogan Page.

Linman, Jonathan (2010), *Holy Conversation: Spirituality for Worship*, Minneapolis, MN: Fortress Press.

McGrath, Alister (2008), *The Christian Vision of God*, London: SPCK.

McIntosh, Mark A. (2008), *Divine Teaching: An Introduction to Christian Theology*, Oxford: Blackwell.

Macy, Joanna and Brown, Molly Young (2013), *Coming Back to Life: Practices to Reconnect Our Lives, Our World*, Gabriola Island, BC: New Society Publishers.

Manney, Jim (2011), *A Simple Life-Changing Prayer: Discovering the Power of St Ignatius Loyola's Examen*, Chicago: Loyola Press.

Marshall, Judi, Coleman, Gill and Reason, Peter (2011), *Leadership for Sustainability: An Action Research Approach*, Sheffield: Greenleaf Publishing.

Marti, Gerardo and Ganiel, Gladys (2014), *The Deconstructed Church: Understanding Emerging Christianity*, Oxford: Oxford University Press.

Mudge, Lewis S. and Poling, James N. (eds) (2009), *Formation and Reflection: The Promise of Practical Theology*, Minneapolis, MN: Fortress Press.

Müller, Peter and de Aránguiz, Angel Fernández (2010), *Every Pilgrim's Guide to Walking to Santiago de Compostela*, trans. Laurie Dennet, Norwich: Canterbury Press.

Orsuto, Donna (2006), *Holiness*, London: Continuum.

Palmer, Parker J. (2008), *The Promise of Paradox: A Celebration of Contradictions in the Christian Life*, San Francisco, CA: Jossey-Bass.

Parker, Russ (2014), *Rediscovering the Ministry of Blessing*, London: SPCK.

Pickard, Jan Sutch (2001), 'Dreams and Visions: A Blessing', in Ruth Burgess (ed.), *A Book of Blessings: And How to Write your Own*, Glasgow: Wild Goose.

Pickard, Stephen (2012), *Seeking the Church: An Introduction to Ecclesiology*, London: SCM Press.

Quash, Ben (2013), *Found Theology: History, Imagination and the Holy Spirit*, London: T. & T. Clark.

Quiller-Couch, Arthur (ed.) (1919), *The Oxford Book of English Verse: 1250–1900*, Oxford: Oxford University Press.

Reason, Peter and Torbert, William R. (2001), 'The Action Turn: Toward a Transformational Social Science', *Concepts and Transformations* 6:1, pp. 1–37.

Reason, P. and Bradbury, H. (2008), 'Introduction', in P. Reason and H. Bradbury (eds), *Handbook of Action Research*, London: Sage.

Redekop, Benjamin W. (ed.) (2010), *Leadership for Environmental Sustainability*, New York and London: Routledge.

Rifkin, F. (2010), *The Ethics of Participatory Theatre in Higher Education: A Framework for Learning and Teaching*, York: The Higher Education Academy and Palatine Drama, Dance and Music – <www.heacademy.ac.uk/resources/details/subjects/palatine/ethics-of-participatory-theatre>.

Robinson, Anthony B. (2008), *Changing the Conversation: A Third Way for Congregations*, Cambridge: Eerdmans.

Rohr, Richard (2012), 'The Eight Core Principles', *Radical Grace* 25:4, Fall 2012, pp. 43–4.

Rohr, Richard (2014), *Great Themes of Paul: Life as Participants*, Disc 1 (audiobook), Center for Action and Contemplation, <store.cac.org>.

Saramago, José (2012), *Raised from the Ground*, trans. Margaret Jull Costa, London: Harvill Secker.

Scharmer, Otto C. (2009), *Theory U: Leading from the Future as it Emerges – The Social Technology of Presencing*, San Francisco, CA: Berrett-Koehler.

Scharmer, Otto C. and Kaufer, Katrin (2013), *Leading from the Emerging Future: From Ego-System to Eco-System Economies*, San Francisco, CA: Berrett-Koehler.

Short, Nigel P., Turner, Lydia and Grant, Alec (eds) (2013), *Contemporary British Autoethnography*, Rotterdam: Sense Publishers.

Stapley, Lionel F. (1996), *The Personality of the Organisation: A Psycho-Dynamic Explanation of Culture and Change*, London and New York: Free Association Books.

Thorne, Brian (1991), *Person-Centred Counselling: Therapeutic and Spiritual Dimensions*, London: Whurr Publications.

Thornton, Martin (1968), *The Function of Theology*, New York: Seabury Press.

Tomlin, Graham (2014), *The Widening Circle: Priesthood as God's Way of Blessing the World*, London: SPCK.

Torbert, Bill (1991), *The Power of Balance: Transforming Self, Society, and Scientific Inquiry*, Newbury Park, CA: Sage.

Torbert, Bill (2004), *Action Inquiry: The Secret of Timely and Transforming Leadership*, San Francisco, CA: Berrett-Koehler.

Treier, Daniel J. (2006), *Virtue and the Voice of God: Towards Theology as Wisdom*, Grand Rapids, MN and Cambridge: Eerdmans.

Vanier, Jean (2004), *Drawn into the Mystery of Jesus through the Gospel of John*, London: Darton, Longman & Todd.

Vanier, Jean (1988, 2009), *The Broken Body: Journey to Wholeness*, London: Darton, Longman & Todd.

Vanier, Jean (2012), *Community and Growth*, London: Darton, Longman & Todd.

Volf, Miroslav (2010), *Against the Tide: Love in a Time of Petty Dreams and Persisting Enmities*, Cambridge: Eerdmans.

Voorwinde, Stephen (2011), *Jesus' Emotions in the Gospels*, London: T. and T. Clark.

Walter, Gregory (2013), *Being Promised: Theology, Gift and Practice*, Cambridge: Eerdmans.

Wells, Jo Bailey (2000), *God's Holy People: A Theme in Biblical Theology*, *Journal for the Study of the Old Testament*, Supplement Series 305, Sheffield: Sheffield Academic Press.

Wells, Samuel (2006), *God's Companions: Reimagining Christian Ethics*, Oxford: Blackwell.

Wells, Samuel (2013), *Learning to Dream Again: Rediscovering the Heart of God*, Norwich: Canterbury Press.

Wheatley, Margaret J. (1999), *Leadership and the New Science: Discovering Order in a Chaotic World*, San Francisco, CA: Berrett-Koehler.

Wheatley, Margaret J. (2002), *Turning to One Another*, San Francisco, CA: Berrett-Koehler.

Wheatley, Margaret J. (2012), *So Far From Home: Lost and Found in Our Brave New World*, San Francisco, CA: Berrett-Koehler.

Wheatley, Margaret J. and Frieze, Deborah (2011), *Walk Out, Walk On: A Learning Journey into Communities Daring to Live the Future Now*, San Francisco, CA: Berrett-Koehler.

Whitney, Diana and Trosten-Bloom, Amanda (2003), *The Power of Appreciative Inquiry: A Practical Guide to Positive Change*, San Francisco, CA: Berrett-Koehler.

Whitney, Diana, Trosten-Bloom, Amanda, Cherney, Jay and Fry, Ron (2004), *Appreciative Team Building: Positive Questions to Bring Out the Best of Your Team*, New York: iUniverse.

Williams, Rowan (2014), *Being Christian: Baptism, Bible, Eucharist, Prayer*, London: SPCK.

Wilson, George B. (2014), 'Leaving "The Church": A Painful Blessing?', *The Way* 53:1, pp. 101–7.

Wimberly, Anne E. Streaty and Parker, Evelyn L. (eds) (2012), *In Search of Wisdom: Faith Formation in the Black Church*, Nashville, TN: Abingdon Press.

Witherington III, Ben (2010), *We Have Seen His Glory: A Vision of Kingdom Worship*, Grand Rapids, MI and Cambridge: Eerdmans.

Woodhead, Linda and Catto, Rebecca (eds) (2012), *Religion and Change in Modern Britain*, Abingdon: Routledge.